PROSPERITY PROMISES

KENNETH & GLORIA COPELAND

Kenneth Copeland Publications
Fort Worth, Texas

Prosperity Promises

ISBN 1-57562-036-7   30-0702

© 1985 Kenneth Copeland Publications

Revised 1997, © 1997 Kenneth and Gloria Copeland

All scripture is from the *King James Version,*
The Amplified Bible, The James Moffatt Translation and
the *New International Version* as noted.

Kenneth Copeland Publications
Fort Worth, Texas 76192-0001

TABLE OF CONTENTS

P R E F A C E

*"Beloved, I wish above all things
that thou mayest prosper and be in health,
even as thy soul prospereth"*
(3 John 2).

When Gloria and I first caught hold of the Word, God helped us understand that the more we fed our spirit the Word, by keeping it going in our ears and in front of our eyes, the stronger our faith would grow. So, we set our hearts to be obedient to the Word. We agreed we would take every truth we saw there and apply it in our lives.

At the time God first started teaching Gloria and me about prosperity, we were up to our necks in $22,000 of debt. We owed so much, for so long, to so many, most of our creditors never expected to get their money. But when we saw some things in the Word about God's laws of prosperity, we made a commitment to pay off those debts and never borrow money again.

For a while it looked like we'd never make it. Our minds gave us fits. But day by day we declared, "God is able." We looked to Him for our deliverance and thanked Him daily for the victory in our finances.

That was nearly 30 years ago, but the principles we learned during that time have held us steady through some turbulent storms in many areas—not just finances. Oftentimes, as believers, our concept of prosperity gets limited to just finances and personal wealth. But God's laws of prosperity govern everything. He wants us to prosper in every area of life—*including* our finances.

To prosper means to succeed and flourish. Prosperity is to advance or gain in anything good or desirable. It also means well-being. Over and over throughout the Scriptures, God reveals that it is His will to prosper His people.

He demonstrated His will in the Garden of Eden when He surrounded Adam and Eve with every material blessing they could possibly need. He proved it again when He prospered His friend Abraham almost beyond belief. God's desire to bless His people is repeatedly evident in His dealings with the Israelite nation. Has God changed since then? No. The Bible says He is the same yesterday, today and forever (Hebrews 13:8).

Godly prosperity operates by putting God's Word in our heart, keeping it coming out of our mouth, while we continue building our lives upon it. What excites me so much about God's principles of prosperity is they'll work any time, anywhere for anyone.

The law of sowing and reaping, for example, is a powerful force. Its principle of giving governs everything in the kingdom of God and is fundamental to godly prosperity. Faith in the Word of God coupled with giving will always produce a harvest of prosperity. Always.

Good stewardship is another principle that is key to our financial increase. God expects us to be faithful stewards of everything He entrusts to us. But primarily, God requires us to be faithful stewards of His anointing. When we're faithful stewards of the anointing, we'll walk in love to guard its effectiveness in our life. We'll walk by faith to keep the anointing flowing strong. A good steward of the anointing also knows that money isn't for hoarding—money is for giving. He doesn't love money—he loves people. He uses money to bless people.

When you live like that, God will see to it that you have all the money you need. Why? Because God's priority is to destroy yokes and remove burdens by the power of His anointing through you. He desires to bless His people. And when your life lines up with God's priority, He'll see to it that you prosper spiritually, physically, financially and any other way you can think.

This book will show you what the Scriptures say about prosperity from God. Read it. Meditate on it. Carry it with you. Take the time to saturate your spirit and mind in these exceeding great and precious promises. They'll increase your faith and cause you to partake of the divine nature of God. *That* in itself is to prosper greatly.

Kenneth and Gloria Copeland

Prosperity Is
God's Will

You don't have to talk God into the idea of prospering you. Since the Garden of Eden, prosperity and blessing have been His idea.

Many times in the Bible, God promises His people that He will bless them. And that word "bless" encompasses a wide range of good things that He wants to do for us. In *Vine's Expository Dictionary of Biblical Words*, "bless" is defined as "to prosper, to make happy, to bestow blessings on." *Webster's Dictionary* defines "bless" as "to set apart or consecrate for holy purposes, to make and pronounce holy, to make happy, to make successful, to make prosperous in temporal concerns or pertaining to this life, to keep, to guard, to preserve."

God has always prospered His people. He made the earth for mankind—for His people. He delights and takes great pleasure in prospering you. As you study the Scriptures, you'll see that it is clearly God's will for you to prosper spiritually, mentally, physically and financially.

He wants you to experience His abundant provision in *every* area of your life. When you believe God is not only *able*, but also *willing* to meet all your needs, your life will overflow with the abundant blessings He always intended for you to enjoy.

Deuteronomy 7:13

KJV—He will love thee, and bless thee, and multiply thee: he will also bless the fruit of thy womb, and the fruit of thy land, thy corn, and thy wine, and thine oil, the increase of thy kine, and the flocks of thy sheep, in the land which he sware unto thy fathers to give thee.

Amp—He will love you, bless you, and multiply you; He will also bless the fruit of your body and the fruit of your land, your grain, your new wine, and your oil, the increase of your cattle and the young of your flock, in the land which He swore to your fathers to give you.

Moffatt—He will love you, prosper you, and multiply you, he will prosper the fruit of your womb and the fruit of your ground, your corn and wine and oil, the young of your cattle and the lambs of your flock, in the land which he swore to your fathers that he would give to you.

NIV—He will love you and bless you and increase your numbers. He will bless the fruit of your womb, the crops of your land—your grain, new wine and oil—the calves of your herds and the lambs of your flocks in the land that he swore to your forefathers to give you.

1 Chronicles 29:11-12

KJV—Thine, O Lord, is the greatness, and the power, and the glory, and the victory, and the majesty: for all that is in the heaven and in the earth is thine; thine is the kingdom, O Lord, and thou art exalted as head above all. Both riches and honour come of thee, and thou reignest over all; and in thine hand is power and might; and in thine hand it is to make great, and to give strength unto all.

Amp—Yours, O Lord, is the greatness, and the power, and the glory, and the victory, and the majesty; for all that is in the heavens and the earth is Yours; Yours is the Kingdom, O Lord, and Yours it is to be exalted as head over all. Both riches and honor come from You, and You reign over all. In Your hand are power and might; in

Prosperity Is God's Will

Your hand it is to make great and to give strength to all.

Moffatt—Thine, O Eternal, is the greatness and the power and the glory and the pre-eminence and the majesty, for all in heaven and earth is thine; thine is the dominion, O Eternal, and thine the supreme authority! Riches and honour come from thee, who reignest over all; in thy hand lie power and might, and in thy hand it lies to make all great and strong.

NIV—Yours, O Lord, is the greatness and the power and the glory and the majesty and the splendor, for everything in heaven and earth is yours. Yours, O Lord, is the kingdom; you are exalted as head over all. Wealth and honor come from you; you are the ruler of all things. In your hands are strength and power to exalt and give strength to all.

Psalm 23:1

KJV—The Lord is my shepherd; I shall not want.

Amp—The Lord is my shepherd [to feed, guide and shield me]; I shall not lack.

Moffatt—The Eternal shepherds me, I lack for nothing.

NIV—The Lord is my shepherd, I shall not be in want.

Psalm 35:27

KJV—Let them shout for joy, and be glad, that favour my righteous cause: yea, let them say continually, Let the Lord be magnified, which hath pleasure in the prosperity of his servant.

Amp—Let those who favor my righteous cause and have pleasure in my uprightness shout for joy and be glad, and say continually, Let the Lord be magnified, Who takes pleasure in the prosperity of His servant.

Moffatt—May they shout for joy, may they be glad, who love to see me righted! May they have ever cause to say, "All hail to the Eternal, who loves to see his servant prospering!"

NIV—May those who delight in my vindication shout for joy and gladness; may they always say, "The Lord be exalted, who delights in the well-being of his servant."

Psalm 37:3-11

KJV—Trust in the Lord, and do good; so shalt thou dwell in the land, and verily thou shalt be fed. Delight thyself also in the Lord;

and he shall give thee the desires of thine heart. Commit thy way unto the Lord; trust also in him; and he shall bring it to pass. And he shall bring forth thy righteousness as the light, and thy judgment as the noonday.

Rest in the Lord, and wait patiently for him: fret not thyself because of him who prospereth in his way, because of the man who bringeth wicked devices to pass. Cease from anger, and forsake wrath: fret not thyself in any wise to do evil. For evildoers shall be cut off: but those that wait upon the Lord, they shall inherit the earth.

For yet a little while, and the wicked shall not be: yea, thou shalt diligently consider his place, and it shall not be. But the meek shall inherit the earth; and shall delight themselves in the abundance of peace.

Amp—Trust (lean on, rely on and be confident) in the Lord, and do good; so shall you dwell in the land and feed surely on His faithfulness, and truly you shall be fed. Delight yourself also in the Lord, and He will give you the desires and secret petitions of your heart. Commit your way to the Lord—roll and repose [each care of] your load on Him; trust (lean on, rely on and be confident) also in Him, and He will bring it to pass. And He will make your uprightness and right standing with God go forth as the light, and your justice and right as [the shining sun of] the noonday.

Be still and rest in the Lord; wait for Him, and patiently stay yourself upon Him; fret not yourself because of him who prospers in his way, because of the man who brings wicked devices to pass. Cease from anger and forsake wrath; fret not yourself; it tends only to evil-doing. For evildoers shall be cut off; but those who wait and hope and look for the Lord, [in the end] shall inherit the earth.

For yet a little while and the evildoer will be no more; though you look with care where he used to be, he will not be found. But the meek [in the end] shall inherit the earth, and shall delight themselves in the abundance of peace.

Moffatt—Trust in the Eternal and do right, be loyal to him within his land; make the Eternal your delight, and he will give you all your heart's desire. Leave all to him, rely on him, and he will see to it; he will bring your innocence to light, and make the justice of your cause clear as noonday.

Leave it to the Eternal and be patient; fret not over the successful man, who aims to slay the upright, and carries out his wicked plan. Cease your anger, give up raging, fret not—it only leads to evil. Evildoers shall indeed be rooted out, and the land left to those who wait for the Eternal.

A little longer, and the godless will be gone; look in his haunts, and he is there no more! The land will be left to the humble, to enjoy plenteous prosperity.

NIV—Trust in the Lord and do good; dwell in the land and enjoy safe pasture. Delight yourself in the Lord and he will give you the desires of your heart. Commit your way to the Lord; trust in him and he will do this: He will make your righteousness shine like the dawn, the justice of your cause like the noonday sun.

Be still before the Lord and wait patiently for him; do not fret when men succeed in their ways, when they carry out their wicked schemes. Refrain from anger and turn from wrath; do not fret—it leads only to evil. For evil men will be cut off, but those who hope in the Lord will inherit the land.

A little while, and the wicked will be no more; though you look for them, they will not be found. But the meek will inherit the land and enjoy great peace.

Psalm 37:25-26

KJV—I have been young, and now am old; yet have I not seen the righteous forsaken, nor his seed begging bread. He is ever merciful, and lendeth; and his seed is blessed.

Amp—I have been young and now am old, yet have I not seen the [uncompromisingly] righteous forsaken or his seed begging bread. All day long he is merciful and deals graciously; he lends, and his offspring is blessed.

Moffatt—I have been young and I am old, but never have I seen good men forsaken; they always have something to give away, something wherewith to bless their families.

NIV—I was young and now I am old, yet I have never seen the righteous forsaken or their children begging bread. They are always generous and lend freely; their children will be blessed.

Psalm 84:1-12

KJV—How amiable are thy tabernacles, O Lord of hosts! My soul longeth, yea, even fainteth for the courts of the Lord: my heart and my flesh crieth out for the living God. Yea, the sparrow hath found an house, and the swallow a nest for herself, where she may lay her young, even thine altars, O Lord of hosts, my King, and my God.

Blessed are they that dwell in thy house: they will be still praising thee. Selah. Blessed is the man whose strength is in thee; in whose heart are the ways of them. Who passing through the valley of Baca make it a well; the rain also filleth the pools. They go from strength to strength, every one of them in Zion appeareth before God.

O Lord God of hosts, hear my prayer: give ear, O God of Jacob. Selah. Behold, O God our shield, and look upon the face of thine anointed. For a day in thy courts is better than a thousand. I had rather be a doorkeeper in the house of my God, than to dwell in the tents of wickedness.

For the Lord God is a sun and shield: the Lord will give grace and glory: no good thing will he withhold from them that walk uprightly. O Lord of hosts, blessed is the man that trusteth in thee.

Amp—How lovely are Your tabernacles, O Lord of hosts! My soul yearns, yes, even pines and is homesick for the courts of the Lord; my heart and my flesh cry out and sing for joy to the living God. Yes, the sparrow has found a house, and the swallow a nest for herself, where she may lay her young, even Your altars, O Lord of hosts, my King and my God.

Blessed—happy, fortunate [to be envied]—are those who dwell in Your house and Your presence; they will be singing Your praises all the day long. Selah [pause, and calmly think of that]. Blessed—happy, fortunate [to be envied]—is the man whose strength is in You; in whose heart are the highways to Zion. Passing through the valley of weeping they make it a place of springs; the early rain also fills [the pools] with blessings. They go from strength to strength—increasing in victorious power; each of them appears before God in Zion.

O Lord God of hosts, hear my prayer; give ear, O God of Jacob! Selah [pause, and calmly think of that]! Behold our shield [the king as Your agent], O God, and look upon the face of Your anointed! For a day in Your courts is better than a thousand [anywhere else]; I had rather be a doorkeeper and stand at the threshold in the house of my God than to dwell [at ease] in the tents of wickedness.

For the Lord God is a sun and shield; the Lord bestows [present] grace and favor and [future] glory—honor, splendor and heavenly bliss! No good thing will He withhold from those who walk uprightly. O Lord of hosts, blessed—happy, fortunate [to be envied]—is the man who trusts in You, (leaning and believing on You, committing all and confidently looking to You, and that without fear or misgiving)!

Moffatt—How dear thy dwelling is, O Lord of hosts! My soul has been panting, pining for the courts of the Eternal; now soul and body thrill with joy over the living God, over thine own altars, O Lord of hosts, my King, my God; the bird has found her home at last, a nest to lay her young!

Happy are they who live within thy house, praising thee all day long! Happy are they who, nerved by thee, set out on

*Prosperity
Is God's Will*

pilgrimage! When they pass through Wearyglen, fountains flow for their refreshing, blessings rain upon them; they are stronger as they go, till God at last reveals himself in Sion.

Hear my prayer, O Lord of hosts, O God of Jacob, listen; God, our protector, look on us, welcome thy chosen to thy presence. Better a single day within thy courts than a thousand days outside! I would rather sit at the threshold of God's house than live inside the tents of worldly men.

For God the Eternal is a sun and shield, favour and honour he bestows; he never denies bliss to the upright. O Lord of hosts, happy the man who trusts in thee.

NIV—How lovely is your dwelling place, O Lord Almighty! My soul yearns, even faints, for the courts of the Lord; my heart and my flesh cry out for the living God. Even the sparrow has found a home, and the swallow a nest for herself, where she may have her young—a place near your altar, O Lord Almighty, my King and my God.

Blessed are those who dwell in your house; they are ever praising you. Selah. Blessed are those whose strength is in you, who have set their hearts on pilgrimage. As they pass through the Valley of Baca, they make it a place of springs; the autumn rains also cover it with pools. They go from

strength to strength, till each appears before God in Zion.

Hear my prayer, O Lord God Almighty;
listen to me, O God of Jacob. Selah. Look
upon our shield, O God; look with favor on
your anointed one. Better is one day in your
courts than a thousand elsewhere; I would
rather be a doorkeeper in the house of my
God than dwell in the tents of the wicked.

For the Lord God is a sun and shield; the
Lord bestows favor and honor; no good
thing does he withhold from those whose
walk is blameless. O Lord Almighty, blessed
is the man who trusts in you.

Psalm 85:12

KJV—Yea, the Lord shall give that which is
good; and our land shall yield her increase.

Amp—Yes, the Lord will give what is good,
and our land will yield its increase.

Moffatt—Yes, the Eternal brings us bliss;
our land is yielding fruit.

NIV—The Lord will indeed give what is
good, and our land will yield its harvest.

Psalm 92:12-15

KJV—The righteous shall flourish like the
palm tree: he shall grow like a cedar in

Lebanon. Those that be planted in the house of the Lord shall flourish in the courts of our God. They shall still bring forth fruit in old age; they shall be fat and flourishing; To show that the Lord is upright: he is my rock, and there is no unrighteousness in him.

Amp—The [uncompromisingly] righteous shall flourish like the palm tree [be long-lived, stately, upright, useful and fruitful]; he shall grow like a cedar in Lebanon [majestic, stable, durable and incorruptible]. Planted in the house of the Lord, they shall flourish in the courts of our God. [Growing in grace] they shall still bring forth fruit in old age; they shall be full of sap [of spiritual vitality] and rich in the verdure [of trust, love and contentment]. [They are living memorials] to show that the Lord is upright and faithful to His promises; He is my rock, and there is no unrighteousness in Him.

Moffatt—Good men flourish like a palm, and grow like cedars on Lebânon; planted inside the Eternal's precincts, they flourish in the courts of our God, still bearing fruit when they are old, still fresh and green—showing how just the Eternal is, my Strength who never errs.

NIV—The righteous will flourish like a palm tree, they will grow like a cedar of

Lebanon; planted in the house of the Lord, they will flourish in the courts of our God. They will still bear fruit in old age, they will stay fresh and green, proclaiming, "The Lord is upright; he is my Rock, and there is no wickedness in him."

Psalm 115:11-16

KJV—Ye that fear the Lord, trust in the Lord: he is their help and their shield. The Lord hath been mindful of us: he will bless us; he will bless the house of Israel; he will bless the house of Aaron. He will bless them that fear the Lord, both small and great. The Lord shall increase you more and more, you and your children. Ye are blessed of the Lord which made heaven and earth. The heaven, even the heavens, are the Lord's: but the earth hath he given to the children of men.

Amp—You who (reverently) fear the Lord, trust and lean on the Lord! He is their help and their shield. The Lord has been mindful of us; He will bless us; He will bless the house of Israel; He will bless the house of Aaron [the priesthood]. He will bless those who reverently and worshipfully fear the Lord, both small and great. The Lord give you increase more and more, you and your children. Blessed be you of the Lord, Who made Heaven and earth! The heavens are

Prosperity Is God's Will

the Lord's heavens, but the earth has He given to the children of men.

Moffatt—The Eternal's worshippers trust in the Eternal; he is their shield and succour. The Eternal remembers us, and he will bless us, he will bless Israel and Aaron's household, he will bless his worshippers, both high and low alike. The Eternal will make you increase, will multiply you and your children. Your blessing comes from the Eternal, who made heaven and earth, the heaven that the Eternal holds himself, the earth he has assigned to men.

NIV—You who fear him, trust in the Lord— he is their help and shield. The Lord remembers us and will bless us: He will bless the house of Israel, he will bless the house of Aaron, he will bless those who fear the Lord—small and great alike. May the Lord make you increase, both you and your children. May you be blessed by the Lord, the Maker of heaven and earth. The highest heavens belong to the Lord, but the earth he has given to man.

Psalm 145:8-9

KJV—The Lord is gracious, and full of compassion; slow to anger, and of great mercy. The Lord is good to all: and his tender mercies are over all his works.

Amp—The Lord is gracious and full of compassion, slow to anger and abounding in mercy and loving-kindness. The Lord is good to all, and His tender mercies are over all His works—the entirety of things created.

Moffatt—The Eternal is gracious and pitiful, slow to be angry, very kind; the Eternal is good to all who look to him, and his compassion covers all that he has made.

NIV—The Lord is gracious and compassionate, slow to anger and rich in love. The Lord is good to all; he has compassion on all he has made.

Proverbs 8:17-21

KJV—I love them that love me; and those that seek me early shall find me. Riches and honour are with me; yea, durable riches and righteousness. My fruit is better than gold, yea, than fine gold; and my revenue than choice silver. I lead in the way of righteousness, in the midst of the paths of judgment: That I may cause those that love me to inherit substance; and I will fill their treasures.

Amp—I love those who love me, and those who seek me early and diligently shall find me. Riches and honor are with me, enduring wealth, and righteousness [that is, uprightness in every area and relation, and right standing with God]. My fruit is better than gold, yes, than refined gold, and my increase than choice silver. [Wisdom] walk in the way of righteousness [of moral and spiritual rectitude in every area and relation], in the midst of the paths of justice, That I may cause those who love me to inherit [true] riches, and that I may fill their treasuries.

Moffatt—Those who love me, I love them; those who seek me find me. I hold wealth and honour, position and good fortune; what I yield is better than the best of gold, what I bring in is better than rare silver. I deal right fairly, justly do I act, enriching those who love me, and filling their stores full.

NIV—I love those who love me, and those who seek me find me. With me are riches and honor, enduring wealth and prosperity. My fruit is better than fine gold; what I yield surpasses choice silver. I walk in the way of righteousness, along the paths of justice, bestowing wealth on those who love me and making their treasuries full.

Ecclesiastes 5:19

KJV—Every man also to whom God hath given riches and wealth, and hath given him power to eat thereof...and to rejoice in his labour; this is the gift of God.

Amp—Every man to whom God has given riches and possessions and power to enjoy them...and to rejoice in his toil, this is the gift of God to him.

Moffatt—It is God's own gift when a man is made rich and wealthy and able to enjoy it all...and to enjoy himself as he toils.

NIV—When God gives any man wealth and possessions, and enables him to enjoy them...and be happy in his work—this is a gift of God.

Jeremiah 29:11

KJV—For I know the thoughts that I think toward you, saith the Lord, thoughts of peace, and not of evil, to give you an expected end.

Amp—For I know the thoughts and plans that I have for you, says the Lord, thoughts and plans for welfare and peace, and not for evil, to give you hope in your final outcome.

Moffatt—For I keep in mind my purpose for you, a purpose of weal, not of woe, to let you have hope for the future.

NIV—"For I know the plans I have for you," declares the Lord, "plans to prosper you and not to harm you, plans to give you hope and a future."

Acts 14:17

KJV—He [God] left not himself without witness, in that he did good, and gave us rain from heaven, and fruitful seasons, filling our hearts with food and gladness.

Amp—He [God] did not neglect to leave some witness of Himself, for He did you good and kindnesses, and gave you rains from heaven and fruitful seasons, satisfying your hearts with nourishment and happiness.

Moffatt—As the bountiful Giver he [God] did not leave himself without a witness, giving you rain from heaven and fruitful seasons, giving you food and joy to your heart's content.

NIV—He [God] has not left himself without testimony: He has shown kindness by giving you rain from heaven and crops in their seasons; he provides you with plenty of food and fills your hearts with joy.

Romans 8:32

KJV—He that spared not his own Son, but delivered him up for us all, how shall he not with him also freely give us all things?

Amp—He who did not withhold or spare [even] His own Son but gave Him up for us all, will He not also with Him freely and graciously give us all [other] things?

Moffatt—The God who did not spare his own son but gave him up for us all, surely He will give us everything besides!

NIV—He who did not spare his own Son, but gave him up for us all—how will he not also, along with him, graciously give us all things?

James 1:17

KJV—Every good gift and every perfect gift is from above, and cometh down from the Father of lights, with whom is no variableness, neither shadow of turning.

Amp—Every good gift and every perfect (free, large, full) gift is from above; it comes down from the Father of all [that gives] light, in [the shining of] Whom there can be no variation [rising or setting] or shadow cast by His turning [as in an eclipse].

Moffatt—Make no mistake about this, my beloved brothers: all we are given is good, and all our endowments are faultless, descending from above, from the Father of the heavenly lights, who knows no change of rising and setting, who casts no shadow on the earth.

NIV—Every good and perfect gift is from above, coming down from the Father of the heavenly lights, who does not change like shifting shadows.

3 John 2

KJV—Beloved, I wish above all things that thou mayest prosper and be in health, even as thy soul prospereth.

Amp—Beloved, I pray that you may prosper in every way and [that your body] may keep well, even as [I know] your soul keeps well and prospers.

Moffatt—Beloved, I pray you may prosper in every way and keep well—as indeed your soul is keeping well.

NIV—Dear friend, I pray that you may enjoy good health and that all may go well with you, even as your soul is getting along well.

Prosperity's Principles
and Foundation

When it comes to prosperity, the Word of God is the secret to your success. But just reading the Word isn't what makes you successful.

When God instructed Joshua about what to do to become prosperous and have good success, He told Joshua three things to do with the Word on a continual, night-and-day basis. He said to speak the Word, meditate on the Word, and do (obey) the Word (Joshua 1:7-8).

When we get actively involved with the Word, allowing it to fill our thoughts, direct our conversation and determine our actions, that's when we really become doers of the Word. And God promised us, the doer of His Word is who will be prosperous and blessed.

Leviticus 26:3-5

KJV—If ye walk in my statutes, and keep my commandments, and do them; Then I will give you rain in due season, and the land shall yield her increase, and the trees of the field shall yield their fruit. And your threshing shall reach unto the vintage, and the vintage shall reach unto the sowing time: and ye shall eat your bread to the full, and dwell in your land safely.

Amp—If you walk in My statutes and keep My commandments and do them, I will give you rain in due season, and the land shall yield her increase, and the trees of the field yield their fruit. And your threshing [time] shall reach to the vintage, and the vintage [time] shall reach to the sowing time; and you shall eat your bread to the full, and dwell in your land securely.

Moffatt—If you live by my rules and follow my orders obediently, I will give you the rains in due season, the land shall bear its crops, the trees shall bear their fruit; your threshing shall last till the time for vintage, and your vintage shall last till the time for sowing; you shall have plenty to eat and live securely in your land.

NIV—If you follow my decrees and are careful to obey my commands, I will send you rain in its season, and the ground will yield its crops and the trees of the field their fruit. Your threshing will continue until grape harvest and the grape harvest will continue until planting, and you will eat all the food you want and live in safety in your land.

Leviticus 27:30

KJV—All the tithe of the land, whether of the seed of the land, or of the fruit of the tree, is the Lord's: it is holy unto the Lord.

Amp—All the tithe of the land, whether of the seed of the land or of the fruit of the tree, is the Lord's; it is holy to the Lord.

Moffatt—The tithe of all the land, whether in grain from the field or in fruit from the tree, all belongs to the Eternal; it is sacred to the Eternal.

NIV—A tithe of everything from the land, whether grain from the soil or fruit from the trees, belongs to the Lord; it is holy to the Lord.

Deuteronomy 6:1-3

KJV—Now these are the commandments, the statutes, and the judgments, which the Lord your God commanded to teach you,

Prosperity's Principles and Foundation

that ye might do them in the land whither ye go to possess it: That thou mightest fear the Lord thy God, to keep all his statutes and his commandments, which I command thee, thou, and thy son, and thy son's son, all the days of thy life; and that thy days may be prolonged. Hear therefore, O Israel, and observe to do it; that it may be well with thee, and that ye may increase mightily, as the Lord God of thy fathers hath promised thee, in the land that floweth with milk and honey.

Amp—Now this is the instruction, the laws, and the precepts, which the Lord your God commanded me to teach you, that you might do them in the land to which you go to possess it; That you may (reverently) fear the Lord your God, you and your son and your son's son, and keep all His statutes and His commandments, which I command you, all the days of your life; and that your days may be prolonged. Hear therefore, O Israel, and be watchful to do them; that it may be well with you, and that you may increase exceedingly as the Lord God of your fathers has promised you, in a land flowing with milk and honey.

Moffatt—Now here is the code, the rules and regulations, which the Eternal your God has directed that you are to be taught to follow in the land which you are crossing to make your own, a land abounding with milk and honey, that you may reverence the Eternal your God by obeying all his rules and orders all your life, as I enjoin them upon you and your sons and your grandsons, that you may have a long life. Listen then, Israel, and be mindful to obey, that things may go well with you, and that you may multiply greatly, as the Eternal the God of your fathers has promised you.

NIV—These are the commands, decrees and laws the Lord your God directed me to teach you to observe in the land that you are crossing the Jordan to possess, So that you, your children and their children after them may fear the Lord your God as long as you live by keeping all his decrees and commands that I give you, and so that you may enjoy long life. Hear, O Israel, and be careful to obey so that it may go well with you and that you may increase greatly in a land flowing with milk and honey, just as the Lord, the God of your fathers, promised you.

Deuteronomy 28:1-2

KJV—It shall come to pass, if thou shalt hearken diligently unto the voice of the Lord thy God, to observe and to do all his commandments which I command thee this day, that the Lord thy God will set thee on high above all nations of the earth: And all these blessings shall come on thee, and overtake thee, if thou shalt hearken unto the voice of the Lord thy God.

Amp—If you will listen diligently to the voice of the Lord your God, being watchful to do all His commandments which I command you this day, the Lord your God will set you high above all the nations of the earth, And all these blessings shall come upon you and overtake you, if you heed the voice of the Lord your God.

Moffatt—If only you will listen carefully to what the Eternal your God orders, mindful to carry out all his commands which I enjoin upon you this day, then the Eternal your God will lift you high above all the nations of the earth, and all these blessings shall come upon you and overtake you, if only you listen to the voice of the Eternal your God.

NIV—If you fully obey the Lord your God and carefully follow all his commands I give you today, the Lord your God will set you high above all the nations on earth. All these blessings will come upon you and accompany you if you obey the Lord your God.

Deuteronomy 30:19-20

KJV—I call heaven and earth to record this day against you, that I have set before you life and death, blessing and cursing: therefore choose life, that both thou and thy seed may live: That thou mayest love the Lord thy God, and that thou mayest obey his voice, and that thou mayest cleave unto him: for he is thy life, and the length of thy days: that thou mayest dwell in the land which the Lord sware unto thy fathers, to Abraham, to Isaac, and to Jacob, to give them.

Amp—I call Heaven and earth to witness this day against you, that I have set before you life and death, the blessing and the curse; therefore choose life, that you and your descendants may live; To love the Lord your God, to obey His voice, and to cling to Him; for He is your life, and the length of your days, that you may dwell in the land which the Lord swore to give to your fathers, to Abraham, Isaac, and Jacob.

Moffatt—Here and now I call heaven and earth to witness against you that I have put life and death before you, the blessing and the curse: choose life, then, that you and your children may live, by loving the Eternal your God, obeying his voice, and holding fast to him, for that means life to you and length of days, that you may live in the land which the Eternal swore to Abraham, Isaac, and Jacob, your fathers, that he would give to them.

NIV—This day I call heaven and earth as witnesses against you that I have set before

*Prosperity's
Principles and
Foundation*

you life and death, blessings and curses. Now choose life, so that you and your children may live and that you may love the Lord your God, listen to his voice, and hold fast to him. For the Lord is your life, and he will give you many years in the land he swore to give to your fathers, Abraham, Isaac and Jacob.

Joshua 1:7-8

KJV—Only be thou strong and very courageous, that thou mayest observe to do according to all the law, which Moses my servant commanded thee: turn not from it to the right hand or to the left, that thou mayest prosper whithersoever thou goest.

This book of the law shall not depart out of thy mouth; but thou shalt meditate therein day and night, that thou mayest observe to do according to all that is written therein: for then thou shalt make thy way prosperous, and then thou shalt have good success.

Amp—Only you be strong, and very courageous, that you may do according to all the law, which Moses My servant commanded you. Turn not from it to the right hand or to the left, that you may prosper wherever you go.

This book of the law shall not depart out of your mouth, but you shall meditate on it day and night, that you may observe and do according to all that is written in it; for then you shall make your way prosperous, and then you shall deal wisely and have good success.

Moffatt—Only be strong and brave, mindful to carry out all your orders from my servant Moses, turning neither to the right nor to the left, so that you may succeed wherever you go.

This lawbook you shall never cease to have on your lips; you must pore over it day and night, that you may be mindful to carry out all that is written in it, for so shall you make your way prosperous, so shall you succeed.

NIV—Be strong and very courageous. Be careful to obey all the law my servant Moses gave you; do not turn from it to the right or to the left, that you may be successful wherever you go.

Do not let this Book of the Law depart from your mouth; meditate on it day and night, so that you may be careful to do everything written in it. Then you will be prosperous and successful.

1 Kings 2:3

KJV—Keep the charge of the Lord thy God, to walk in his ways, to keep his statutes, and his commandments, and his judgments, and his testimonies, as it is written in the law of Moses, that thou mayest prosper in all that thou doest, and whithersoever thou turnest thyself.

Amp—Keep the charge of the Lord your God, walk in His ways, keep His statutes, His commandments, His precepts, and His testimonies, as it is written in the law of Moses, that you may do wisely and prosper in all that you do and wherever you turn.

Moffatt—Be strong then, show yourself a man, and do your duty to the Eternal your God, by living his life, by following his rules and orders and regulations and directions, as written in the law of Moses, so that, whatever you do and wherever you turn, you may have success.

NIV—Observe what the Lord your God requires: Walk in his ways, and keep his decrees and commands, his laws and requirements, as written in the Law of Moses, so that you may prosper in all you do and wherever you go.

1 Chronicles 22:13

KJV—Then shalt thou prosper, if thou takest heed to fulfil the statutes and judgments which the Lord charged Moses with concerning Israel: be strong, and of good courage; dread not, nor be dismayed.

Amp—Then you will prosper, if you are careful to keep and fulfill the statutes and ordinances with which the Lord charged Moses concerning Israel. Be strong and of good courage; dread not and fear not; be not dismayed.

Moffatt—If you are mindful to carry out the rules and regulations laid down for Israel by Moses at the bidding of the Eternal, you will succeed. Be firm and brave; never be daunted or dismayed.

NIV—Then you will have success if you are careful to observe the decrees and laws that the Lord gave Moses for Israel. Be strong and courageous. Do not be afraid or discouraged.

2 Chronicles 20:20

KJV—They rose early in the morning, and went forth into the wilderness of Tekoa: and as they went forth, Jehoshaphat stood and said, Hear me, O Judah, and ye inhabitants of Jerusalem; Believe in the Lord your God, so shall ye be established; believe his prophets, so shall ye prosper.

Amp—They rose early in the morning and went out into the wilderness of Tekoa; and as they went out, Jehoshaphat stood and said, Hear me, O Judah, and you inhabitants of Jerusalem! Believe in the Lord your God, and you shall be established; believe and remain steadfast to His prophets, and you shall prosper.

Moffatt—Next morning they rose and moved into the open country round Tekoa. As they advanced, Jehoshaphat stood and said, "Listen, men of Judah and citizens of Jerusalem! Take hold of the Eternal your God and you will keep hold of life; hold by his prophets, and you will prosper."

NIV—Early in the morning they left for the Desert of Tekoa. As they set out, Jehoshaphat stood and said, "Listen to me, Judah and people of Jerusalem! Have faith in the Lord your God and you will be upheld; have faith in his prophets and you will be successful."

2 Chronicles 26:5

KJV—He [Uzziah] sought God in the days of Zechariah, who had understanding in the visions of God: and as long as he sought the Lord, God made him to prosper.

Amp—He [Uzziah] set himself to seek God in the days of Zechariah who instructed him in the things of God; and as long as he sought [inquired of, yearned for] the Lord, God made him prosper.

Moffatt—He [Uzziah] steadily worshipped God during the lifetime of Zechariah, who gave instruction in religion, and as long as he worshipped the Eternal, God gave him success.

NIV—He [Uzziah] sought God during the days of Zechariah, who instructed him in the fear of God. As long as he sought the Lord, God gave him success.

2 Chronicles 31:21

KJV—In every work that he [Hezekiah] began in the service of the house of God, and in the law, and in the commandments, to seek his God, he did it with all his heart, and prospered.

Amp—Every work that he [Hezekiah] began in the service of the house of God, in keeping with the law and the commandments to seek his God, inquiring of and yearning for Him, he did with all his heart, and prospered.

Moffatt—Whatever he [Hezekiah] undertook in the interests of the temple of God, the law, and the commands of God, by way of worshipping his God, he did it with all his heart, and prospered.

NIV—In everything that he [Hezekiah] undertook in the service of God's temple and in obedience to the law and the commands, he sought his God and worked wholeheartedly. And so he prospered.

Job 36:11

KJV—If they [the righteous] obey and serve him [God], they shall spend their days in prosperity, and their years in pleasures.

Amp—If they [the righteous] obey and serve him [God], they shall spend their days in prosperity, and their years in pleasantness and joy.

Moffatt—If they [the righteous] will hear him [God] and submit, they spend a life of prosperous days, and pleasant years.

NIV—If they [the righteous] obey and serve him [God], they will spend the rest of their days in prosperity and their years in contentment.

Psalm 1:1-3

KJV—Blessed is the man that walketh not in the counsel of the ungodly, nor standeth in the way of sinners, nor sitteth in the seat of the scornful. But his delight is in the law of the Lord; and in his law doth he meditate day and night. And he shall be like a tree planted by the rivers of water, that bringeth forth his fruit in his season; his leaf also shall not wither; and whatsoever he doeth shall prosper.

Amp—Blessed—happy, fortunate, prosperous and enviable—is the man who walks and lives not in the counsel of the ungodly [following their advice, their plans and purposes], nor stands [submissive and inactive] in the path where sinners walk, nor sits down [to relax and rest] where the scornful [and the mockers] gather. But his delight and desire are in the law of the Lord, and on His law—the precepts, the instructions, the teachings of God—he habitually meditates (ponders and studies) by day and by night. And he shall be like a tree firmly planted [and tended] by the streams of water, ready to bring forth his fruit in its season; his leaf also shall not fade or wither, and everything he does shall prosper [and come to maturity].

Moffatt—Happy the man who never goes by the advice of the ungodly, who never takes the sinners' road, nor joins the company of scoffers, but finds his joy in the Eternal's law, poring over it day and night. He is like a tree planted by a stream, that bears fruit in due season, with leaves that never fade; whatever he does, he prospers.

Prosperity's Principles and Foundation

NIV—Blessed is the man who does not walk in the counsel of the wicked or stand in the way of sinners or sit in the seat of mockers. But his delight is in the law of the Lord, and on his law he meditates day and night. He is like a tree planted by streams of water, which yields its fruit in season and whose leaf does not wither. Whatever he does prospers.

Psalm 122:6-7

KJV—They shall prosper that love thee. Peace be within thy walls, and prosperity within thy palaces.

Amp—May they prosper that love you |the Holy City|! Peace be within your walls and prosperity within your palaces!

Moffatt—May all thy homes be safe, may all go well within thy walls, within thy palaces!

NIV—May those who love you be secure. May there be peace within your walls and security within your citadels.

Proverbs 3:9-10

KJV—Honour the Lord with thy substance, and with the firstfruits of all thine increase: So shall thy barns be filled with plenty, and thy presses shall burst out with new wine.

Amp—Honor the Lord with your capital and sufficiency [from righteous labors], and with the first fruits of all your income; So shall your storage places be filled with plenty, and your vats be overflowing with new wine.

Moffatt—Honour the Eternal with your wealth, and with the best of all you make; so shall your barns be full of corn, your vats brim over with new wine.

NIV—Honor the Lord with your wealth, with the firstfruits of all your crops; then your barns will be filled to overflowing, and your vats will brim over with new wine.

Proverbs 10:2-6

KJV—Treasures of wickedness profit nothing: but righteousness delivereth from death. The Lord will not suffer the soul of the righteous to famish: but he casteth away the substance of the wicked. He becometh poor that dealeth with a slack hand: but the hand of the diligent maketh rich. He that gathereth in summer is a wise son: but he that sleepeth in harvest is a son that causeth shame. Blessings are upon the head of the just: but violence covereth the mouth of the wicked.

Amp—Treasures of wickedness profit nothing, but righteousness [moral and spiritual rectitude in every area and relation] delivers from death. The Lord will not allow the [uncompromisingly] righteous to famish, but He thwarts the desire of the wicked. He becomes poor who works with a slack and idle hand, but the hand of the diligent makes rich. He who gathers in summer is a wise son, but he who sleeps in harvest is a son who causes shame. Blessings are upon the head of the [uncompromisingly] righteous—the upright, in right standing with God; but the mouth of the wicked conceals violence.

Moffatt—Ill-gotten gains are never a profit: 'tis honesty that ensures life for man. The Eternal never stints an honest man: he thwarts the craving of dishonest men. A slack hand makes men poor: a busy hand makes men rich. He who reaps in summer is a man of sense: he who sleeps through harvest does a shameful thing. God's blessing is upon the good man's head, but the bad man's face shall be darkened with disaster.

NIV—Ill-gotten treasures are of no value, but righteousness delivers from death. The Lord does not let the righteous go hungry but he thwarts the craving of the wicked. Lazy hands make a man poor, but diligent hands bring wealth. He who gathers crops in summer is a wise son, but he who sleeps during harvest is a disgraceful son. Blessings crown the head of the righteous, but violence overwhelms the mouth of the wicked.

Proverbs 11:25

KJV—The liberal soul shall be made fat: and he that watereth shall be watered also himself.

Amp—The liberal person shall be enriched, and he who waters shall himself be watered.

Moffatt—A liberal soul will be enriched, and he who waters will himself be watered.

NIV—A generous man will prosper; he who refreshes others will himself be refreshed.

Proverbs 13:4

KJV—The soul of the sluggard desireth, and hath nothing: but the soul of the diligent shall be made fat.

Amp—The appetite of the sluggard craves and gets nothing, but the appetite of the diligent shall be abundantly supplied.

Moffatt—The lazy man has longings, but gets nothing: the diligent man is amply supplied.

NIV—The sluggard craves and gets nothing, but the desires of the diligent are fully satisfied.

Proverbs 13:11-13

KJV—Wealth gotten by vanity shall be diminished: but he that gathereth by labour shall increase. Hope deferred maketh the heart sick: but when the desire cometh, it is a tree of life. Whoso despiseth the word shall be destroyed: but he that feareth the commandment shall be rewarded.

Amp—Wealth [not earned] but won in haste, or unjustly, or from the production of things for vain or detrimental use, [such riches] will dwindle away; but he who gathers little by little will increase them. Hope deferred makes the heart sick, but when the desire is fulfilled, it is a tree of life. Whoever despises the Word [of God] brings destruction upon himself, but he who (reverently) fears and respects the commandment [of God] shall be rewarded.

Moffatt—Wealth won in haste will dwindle, but, gathered gradually it will grow. Hope deferred is sickening, it is new life to have desire fulfilled. He who despises God's decree shall perish: to stand in awe of God's command is safety.

NIV—Dishonest money dwindles away, but he who gathers money little by little makes it grow. Hope deferred makes the heart sick, but a longing fulfilled is a tree of life. He who scorns instruction will pay for it, but he who respects a command is rewarded.

Proverbs 19:17

KJV—He that hath pity upon the poor lendeth unto the Lord; and that which he hath given will he pay him again.

Amp—He who has pity on the poor lends to the Lord, and that which he has given He will repay to him.

Moffatt—He who cares for the poor is lending to the Eternal, and for his kindness he shall be repaid.

NIV—He who is kind to the poor lends to the Lord, and he will reward him for what he has done.

Proverbs 28:13

KJV—He that covereth his sins shall not prosper: but whoso confesseth and forsaketh them shall have mercy.

Amp—He who covers his transgressions will not prosper, but whoever confesses and forsakes his sins shall obtain mercy.

Moffatt—He who covers up his sins shall never prosper; he who confesses and forsakes them is forgiven.

NIV—He who conceals his sins does not prosper, but whoever confesses and renounces them finds mercy.

Proverbs 28:25

KJV—He that is of a proud heart stirreth up strife: but he that putteth his trust in the Lord shall be made fat.

Amp—He who is of a greedy spirit stirs up strife, but he who puts his trust in the Lord shall be enriched and blessed.

Moffatt—A grasping nature stirs up enmity, but he who trusts in the Eternal thrives.

NIV—A greedy man stirs up dissension, but he who trusts in the Lord will prosper.

Proverbs 28:27

KJV—He that giveth unto the poor shall not lack: but he that hideth his eyes shall have many a curse.

Amp—He who gives to the poor will not want, but he who hides his eyes [from their want] will have many a curse.

Moffatt—A man who helps the poor will never want; he who ignores them will get many a curse.

NIV—He who gives to the poor will lack nothing, but he who closes his eyes to them receives many curses.

Ecclesiastes 11:1

KJV—Cast thy bread upon the waters: for thou shalt find it after many days.

Amp—Cast your bread upon the waters, for you will find it after many days.

Moffatt—Trust your goods far and wide at sea, till you get good returns after a while.

NIV—Cast your bread upon the waters, for after many days you will find it again.

Isaiah 1:19

KJV—If ye be willing and obedient, ye shall eat the good of the land.

Amp—If you are willing and obedient, you shall eat the good of the land.

Moffatt—If only you are willing to obey, you shall feed on the best of the land.

NIV—If you are willing and obedient, you will eat the best from the land.

Isaiah 58:10-11

KJV—If thou draw out thy soul to the hungry, and satisfy the afflicted soul; then shall thy light rise in obscurity, and thy darkness be as the noonday: And the Lord shall guide thee continually, and satisfy thy soul in drought, and make fat thy bones: and thou shalt be like a watered garden, and like a spring of water, whose waters fail not.

Amp—If you pour out that with which you sustain your own life for the hungry, and satisfy the need of the afflicted, then shall your light rise in darkness and your obscurity and gloom be as the noonday. And the Lord shall guide you continually, and satisfy you in drought and in dry places, and make strong your bones. And you shall be like a watered garden and like a spring of water, whose waters fail not.

Moffatt—If you bestow your bread upon the hungry, and relieve men in misery, then light shall dawn for you in darkness, your dull hour shall be bright as noon, and evermore shall the Eternal guide you, guarding you without fail; he will refresh you in dry places, and renew your strength, till you are like a watered garden, like an oasis with a steadfast spring.

NIV—If you spend yourselves in behalf of the hungry and satisfy the needs of the oppressed, then your light will rise in the darkness, and your night will become like the noonday. The Lord will guide you always; he will satisfy your needs in a sun-scorched land and will strengthen your frame. You will be like a well-watered garden, like a spring whose waters never fail.

Jeremiah 17:7-8

KJV—Blessed is the man that trusteth in the Lord, and whose hope the Lord is. For he shall be as a tree planted by the waters, and that spreadeth out her roots by the river, and shall not see when heat cometh, but her leaf shall be green; and shall not be careful in the year of drought, neither shall cease from yielding fruit.

Amp—[Most] blessed is the man who believes in, trusts in and relies on the Lord, and whose hope and confidence the Lord is. For he shall be like a tree planted by the waters, that spreads out its roots by the river, and shall not see and fear when heat comes, but his leaf shall be green; he shall not be

Prosperity's Principles and Foundation

anxious and careful in the year of drought, nor shall he cease from yielding fruit.

Moffatt—But happy he who relies on the Eternal, with the Eternal for his confidence! He is like a tree planted beside a stream, reaching its roots to the water; untouched by any fear of scorching heat, its leaves are ever green, it goes on bearing fruit in days of drought, and lives serene.

NIV—But blessed is the man who trusts in the Lord, whose confidence is in him. He will be like a tree planted by the water that sends out its roots by the stream. It does not fear when heat comes; its leaves are always green. It has no worries in a year of drought and never fails to bear fruit.

Malachi 3:10-12

KJV—Bring ye all the tithes into the storehouse, that there may be meat in mine house, and prove me now herewith, saith the Lord of hosts, if I will not open you the windows of heaven, and pour you out a blessing, that there shall not be room enough to receive it. And I will rebuke the devourer for your sakes, and he shall not destroy the fruits of your ground; neither shall your vine cast her fruit before the time in the field, saith the Lord of hosts. And all nations shall call you blessed: for ye shall be a delightsome land, saith the Lord of hosts.

Amp—Bring all the tithes—the whole tenth of your income—into the storehouse, that there may be food in My house, and prove Me now by it, says the Lord of hosts, if I will not open the windows of Heaven for you and pour you out a blessing, that there shall not be room enough to receive it. And I will rebuke the devourer [insects and plagues] for your sakes, and he shall not destroy the fruits of your ground; neither shall your vine drop its fruit before the time in the field, says the Lord of hosts. And all nations shall call you happy and blessed; for you shall be a land of delight, says the Lord of hosts.

NIV—"Bring the whole tithe into the store-house, that there may be food in my house. Test me in this," says the Lord Almighty, "and see if I will not throw open the flood-gates of heaven and pour out so much blessing that you will not have room enough for it. I will prevent pests from de-vouring your crops, and the vines in your fields will not cast their fruit," says the Lord Almighty. "Then all the nations will call you blessed, for yours will be a delightful land," says the Lord Almighty.

Romans 13:7-8

KJV—Render therefore to all their dues: tribute to whom tribute is due; custom to whom custom; fear to whom fear; honour to whom honour. Owe no man any thing, but to love one another: for he that loveth another hath fulfilled the law.

Amp—Render to all men their dues. [Pay] taxes to whom taxes are due, revenue to whom revenue is due, respect to whom respect is due, and honor to whom honor is due. Keep out of debt and owe no man anything, except to love one another; for he who loves his neighbor—who practices loving others—has fulfilled the Law [relating to one's fellowmen], meeting all its requirements.

Moffatt—Pay them all their respective dues, tribute to one, taxes to another, respect to this man, honour to that, Be in debt to no man—apart from the debt of love one to another. He who loves his fellow-man has fulfilled the law.

NIV—Give everyone what you owe him: If you owe taxes, pay taxes; if revenue, then revenue; if respect, then respect; if honor, then honor. Let no debt remain outstanding, except the continuing debt to love one another, for he who loves his fellowman has fulfilled the law.

1 Corinthians 13:3

KJV—And though I bestow all my goods to feed the poor, and though I give my body to be burned, and have not charity, it profiteth me nothing.

Amp—Even if I dole out all that I have [to the poor in providing] food, and if I surrender my body to be burned [or in order that I may glory], but have not love [God's love in me], I gain nothing.

Moffatt—I may distribute all I possess in charity, I may give up my body to be burnt, but if I have no love, I make nothing of it.

NIV—If I give all I possess to the poor and surrender my body to the flames, but have not love, I gain nothing.

2 Corinthians 9:6-7

KJV—But this I say, He which soweth sparingly shall reap also sparingly; and he which soweth bountifully shall reap also bountifully. Every man according as he purposeth in his heart, so let him give; not grudgingly, or of necessity: for God loveth a cheerful giver.

Amp—[Remember] this: he who sows sparingly and grudgingly will also reap sparingly and grudgingly, and he who sows generously and that blessings may come to someone, will also reap generously and with blessings. Let each one [give] as he has made up his own mind and purposed in his heart, not reluctantly or sorrowfully or under compulsion, for God loves (that is, He takes pleasure in, prizes above other things, and is unwilling to abandon or to do without) a cheerful (joyous, prompt-to-do-it) giver—whose heart is in his giving.

Moffatt—Mark this: he who sows sparingly will reap sparingly, and he who sows generously will reap a generous harvest. Everyone is to give what he has made up his mind to give; there is to be no grudging or compulsion about it, for God loves the giver who gives cheerfully.

NIV—Remember this: Whoever sows sparingly will also reap sparingly, and whoever sows generously will also reap generously. Each man should give what he has decided in his heart to give, not reluctantly or under compulsion, for God loves a cheerful giver.

Galatians 6:6-10

KJV—Let him that is taught in the word communicate unto him that teacheth in all good things. Be not deceived; God is not mocked: for whatsoever a man soweth, that shall he also reap. For he that soweth to his flesh shall of the flesh reap corruption; but he that soweth to the Spirit shall of the Spirit reap life everlasting.

And let us not be weary in well doing: for in due season we shall reap, if we faint not. As we have therefore opportunity, let us do good unto all men, especially unto them who are of the household of faith.

Amp—Let him who receives instruction in the Word |of God| share all good things with his teacher—contributing to his support. Do not be deceived and deluded and misled; God will not allow Himself to be sneered at—scorned, disdained or mocked |by mere pretensions or professions, or His precepts being set aside|.—He inevitably deludes himself who attempts to delude God. For whatever a man sows, that and that only is what he will reap. For he who sows to his own flesh (lower nature, sensuality) will from the flesh reap decay and ruin and destruction; but he who sows to the Spirit will from the Spirit reap life eternal.

And let us not lose heart and grow weary and faint in acting nobly and doing right, for in due time and at the appointed season we shall reap, if we do not loosen and relax our courage and faint. So then, as occasion and opportunity open to us, let us do good (morally) to all people |not only being useful or profitable to them, but also doing what is for their spiritual good and

Prosperity's Principles and Foundation

advantage]. Be mindful to be a blessing, especially to those of the household of faith—those who belong to God's family with you, the believers.

Moffatt—Those who are taught must share all the blessings of life with those who teach them the Word. Make no mistake— God is not to be mocked—a man will reap just what he sows; he who sows for his flesh will reap destruction from the flesh, and he who sows for the Spirit will reap life eternal from the Spirit.

Never let us grow tired of doing what is right, for if we do not faint we shall reap our harvest at the opportune season. So then, as we have opportunity, let us do good to all men and in particular to the household of the faith.

NIV—Anyone who receives instruction in the word must share all good things with his instructor. Do not be deceived: God cannot be mocked. A man reaps what he sows. The one who sows to please his sinful nature, from that nature will reap destruction; the one who sows to please the Spirit, from the Spirit will reap eternal life.

Let us not become weary in doing good, for at the proper time we will reap a harvest if we do not give up. Therefore, as we have opportunity, let us do good to all people, especially to those who belong to the family of believers.

Titus 3:8

KJV—This is a faithful saying, and these things I will that thou affirm constantly, that they which have believed in God might be careful to maintain good works. These things are good and profitable unto men.

Amp—This message is most trustworthy, and concerning these things I want you to insist steadfastly, so that those who have believed in (trusted, relied on) God may be careful to apply themselves to honorable occupations and to doing good, for such things are [not only] excellent and right [in themselves], but [they are] good and profitable for the people.

Moffatt—That is a sure saying. I want you to insist on this, that those who have faith in God make a point of practising honourable occupations. Such counsels are right and good for men.

NIV—This is a trustworthy saying. And I want you to stress these things, so that those who have trusted in God may be careful to devote themselves to doing what is good. These things are excellent and profitable for everyone.

Hebrews 11:6

KJV—Without faith it is impossible to please him: for he that cometh to God must believe that he is, and that he is a rewarder of them that diligently seek him.

Amp—Without faith it is impossible to please and be satisfactory to Him. For whoever would come near to God must (necessarily) believe that God exists and that He is the Rewarder of those who earnestly and diligently seek Him (out).

Moffatt—Apart from faith it is impossible to satisfy him, for the man who draws near to God must believe that he exists and that he does reward those who seek him.

NIV—Without faith it is impossible to please God, because anyone who comes to him must believe that he exists and that he rewards those who earnestly seek him.

Prosperity Is
a Covenant Blessing

When God outlined the terms of His covenant, He guaranteed our physical prosperity in the contract. Over and over He has told us in His Word, "If you do this, I will do this..." In order to withhold material blessings from us, God would have to violate His own covenant agreement, which is impossible for Him to do.

God blesses us with material goods in order for us to establish His covenant on the earth (Deuteronomy 8:18), and to give to those in need. Nothing about God is stingy. Everything about Him is big and generous. He made the streets in heaven out of pure gold! They're not just paved with a gold overlay—they *are* gold!

Besides that, God is a good father. What father, who loves his children, would want to sit in a beautiful, fine mansion, but make his children live in a run-down shack? God isn't opposed to our being rich. That doesn't upset Him even a little. In fact, He delights in our prosperity. He's just opposed to our becoming covetous and greedy. God has a full supply, lacking nothing, and He wants us to be the same way. He wants us to be givers as well—just like He is.

Genesis 13:2, 5-6, 14-17

KJV—Abram was very rich in cattle, in silver, and in gold.... And Lot also, which went with Abram, had flocks, and herds, and tents. And the land was not able to bear them, that they might dwell together: for their substance was great, so that they could not dwell together....

And the Lord said unto Abram, after that Lot was separated from him, Lift up now thine eyes, and look from the place where thou art northward, and southward, and eastward, and westward: For all the land which thou seest, to thee will I give it, and to thy seed for ever. And I will make thy seed as the dust of the earth: so that if a man can number the dust of the earth, then shall thy seed also be numbered. Arise, walk through the land in the length of it and in the breadth of it; for I will give it unto thee.

Amp—Now Abram was extremely rich in livestock and in silver and in gold.... But Lot, who went with Abram, also had flocks and herds and tents. Now the land was not able to nourish and support them so they might dwell together, for their possessions were too great for them to live together....

The Lord said to Abram, after Lot had left him, Lift up now your eyes, and look from the place where you are, northward and southward and eastward and westward; For all the land which you see I will give to you and to your posterity for ever. And I will make your descendants as the dust of the earth, so that if a man can count the dust of the earth, then shall your descendants also be counted. Arise, walk through the land, the length of it and the breadth of it, for I will give it to you.

Moffatt—Abram was very rich in cattle, silver and gold.... Lot, who accompanied Abram, also had flocks and herds and tents. Now the country could not support them both together; their possessions were so large that they could not live side by side....

After Lot had parted from him, the Eternal said to Abram, "Look abroad now from where you are, north, south, east, and west; the land you see, I give it all to you and to your descendants for all time. I will make your descendants as numerous as the dust on the ground, so that if the dust of the ground could be counted your descendants could be counted. Up, traverse the length and breadth of the land, for I give it to you."

NIV—Abram had become very wealthy in livestock and in silver and gold.... Now Lot, who was moving about with Abram, also had flocks and herds and tents. But the land could not support them while they stayed together, for their possessions were so great that they were not able to stay together....

The Lord said to Abram after Lot had parted from him, "Lift up your eyes from where you are and look north and south, east and west. All the land that you see I will give to you and your offspring forever. I will make your offspring like the dust of the earth, so that if anyone could count the dust, then your offspring could be counted. Go, walk through the length and breadth of the land, for I am giving it to you."

Genesis 17:1-9

KJV—When Abram was ninety years old and nine, the Lord appeared to Abram, and said unto him, I am the Almighty God; walk before me, and be thou perfect. And I will make my covenant between me and thee, and will multiply thee exceedingly.

And Abram fell on his face: and God talked with him, saying, As for me, behold, my covenant is with thee, and thou shalt be a father of many nations. Neither shall thy name any more be called Abram, but thy name shall be Abraham; for a father of many nations have I made thee. And I will make thee exceeding fruitful, and I will make nations of thee, and kings shall come out of thee.

And I will establish my covenant between me and thee and thy seed after thee in their generations for an everlasting covenant, to be a God unto thee, and to thy seed after thee. And I will give unto thee, and to thy seed after thee, the land wherein thou art a stranger, all the land of Canaan, for an everlasting possession; and I will be their God. And God said unto Abraham, Thou shalt keep my covenant therefore, thou, and thy seed after thee in their generations.

Amp—When Abram was 99 years old, the Lord appeared to him, and said, I am the Almighty God; walk and live habitually before Me, and be perfect—blameless, wholehearted, complete. And I will make My covenant (solemn pledge) between Me and you, and will multiply you exceedingly.

Then Abram fell on his face; and God said to him, As for Me, behold, My covenant (solemn pledge) is with you, and you shall be the father of many nations. Nor shall your name any longer be Abram (high father), but your name shall be Abraham (father of a multitude); for I have made you the father of many nations. And I will make you exceedingly fruitful, and I will make nations of you, and kings shall come from you.

And I will establish My covenant between Me and you and your descendants after you throughout their generations for an everlasting, solemn pledge to be a God to you and to your posterity after you. And I will give to you and to your posterity after you the land in which you are a stranger (going from place to place), all the land of Canaan for an everlasting possession; and I will be their God. And God said to Abraham, As for you, you shall therefore keep My covenant, you and your descendants after you throughout their generations.

Moffatt—When Abram was ninety-nine, the Eternal appeared to Abram and said, "I am God Almighty; live ever mindful of my presence, and so be blameless; I will make my compact with you and multiply your descendants greatly."

Abram fell on his face; and God continued, "As for me, my compact is made with you, and you shall be the father of many a nation; no longer shall your name be Abram, but Abraham (Many-father), for I have appointed you to be the father of many a nation; I will make you most fruitful, I will make nations out of you, and kings shall spring from you.

"And I will ratify my compact for all time, between me and yourself and your descendants from generation to generation, engaging to be a God to you and to your descendants after you. Also, I will give you and your descendants after you the land where you are residing, the whole of the land of Canaan, as a possession for all time; and I will be their God." God said to Abraham, "As for you, you must keep my compact, you and your descendants after you from generation to generation."

NIV—When Abram was ninety-nine years old, the Lord appeared to him and said, "I am God Almighty; walk before me and be blameless. I will confirm my covenant between me and you and will greatly increase your numbers."

Abram fell facedown, and God said to him, "As for me, this is my covenant with you: You will be the father of many nations. No longer will you be called Abram; your name will be Abraham, for I have made you a father of many nations. I will make you very fruitful; I will make nations of you, and kings will come from you.

"I will establish my covenant as an everlasting covenant between me and you and your descendants after you for the generations to come, to be your God and the God of your descendants after you. The whole land of Canaan, where you are now an alien, I will give as an everlasting possession to you and your descendants after you; and I will be their God." Then God said to

Abraham, "As for you, you must keep my covenant, you and your descendants after you for the generations to come."

Deuteronomy 7:9

KJV—Know therefore that the Lord thy God, he is God, the faithful God, which keepeth covenant and mercy with them that love him and keep his commandments to a thousand generations.

Amp—Know, recognize and understand therefore that the Lord your God, He is God, the faithful God, Who keeps covenant and steadfast love and mercy with those who love Him and keep His commandments, to a thousand generations.

Moffatt—Understand, then, that the Eternal your God is God indeed, a faithful God who carries out his compact of kindness to those who love him and carry out his orders, for a thousand generations.

NIV—Know therefore that the Lord your God is God; he is the faithful God, keeping his covenant of love to a thousand generations of those who love him and keep his commands.

Deuteronomy 8:17-18

KJV—Thou say in thine heart, My power and the might of mine hand hath gotten me this wealth. But thou shalt remember the Lord thy God: for it is he that giveth thee power to get wealth, that he may establish his covenant which he sware unto thy fathers, as it is this day.

Amp—Beware lest you say in your [mind and] heart, My power and the might of my hand have gotten me this wealth. But you shall (earnestly) remember the Lord your God; for it is He Who gives you power to get wealth, that He may establish His covenant which He swore to your fathers, as at this day.

Moffatt—Beware of saying to yourselves, "My own power and the strength of my own hand have won me all this wealth." You must remember the Eternal your God, for it is he who gives you the power of gaining wealth, that he may ratify the compact which he swore to your fathers, as it is today.

NIV—You may say to yourself, "My power and the strength of my hands have produced this wealth for me." But remember the Lord your God, for it is he who gives you the ability to produce wealth, and so

65

Prosperity Is a Covenant Blessing

confirms his covenant, which he swore to
your forefathers, as it is today.

Deuteronomy 11:11-15

KJV—But the land, whither ye go to possess it, is a land of hills and valleys, and
drinketh water of the rain of heaven: A land
which the Lord thy God careth for: the
eyes of the Lord thy God are always upon
it, from the beginning of the year even unto
the end of the year. And it shall come to
pass, if ye shall hearken diligently unto my
commandments which I command you this
day, to love the Lord your God, and to
serve him with all your heart and with all
your soul, That I will give you the rain of
your land in his due season, the first rain
and the latter rain, that thou mayest gather
in thy corn, and thy wine, and thine oil. And
I will send grass in thy fields for thy cattle,
that thou mayest eat and be full.

Amp—But the land, which you enter to
possess, is a land of hills and valleys, and
drinks water of the rain of the heavens; A
land for which the Lord your God cares;
the eyes of the Lord your God are always
upon it, from the beginning of the year to
the end of the year. And if you will diligently heed My commandments which I
command you this day, to love the Lord
your God, and to serve Him with all your

[mind and] heart and with your entire being, I will give the rain for your land in its season, the early rain and the latter rain, that you may gather in your grain, your new wine, and your oil. And I will give grass in your fields for your cattle, that you may eat and be full.

Moffatt—It is a land of hills and valleys, which drinks water as the rain falls, a land for which the Eternal your God cares—the eyes of the Eternal your God are always on it, from the beginning of the year to the end of the year; [[and if you listen carefully to the orders which I enjoin upon you to-day, to love the Eternal your God and worship him with all your mind and all your heart,]] he will give rain to your land at the right season, the spring rains and the autumn rains, that you may gather in your corn and wine and oil, and he will put grass in your fields for your cattle, and you shall eat and be satisfied.

NIV—But the land you are crossing the Jordan to take possession of is a land of mountains and valleys that drinks rain from heaven. It is a land the Lord your God cares for; the eyes of the Lord your God are continually on it from the beginning of the year to its end. So if you faithfully obey the commands I am giving you today—to love the Lord your God and to serve him with all your heart and with all your soul—then I will send rain on your land in its season, both autumn and spring rains, so that you may gather in your grain, new wine and oil. I will provide grass in the fields for your cattle, and you will eat and be satisfied.

Deuteronomy 28:1-14

KJV—It shall come to pass, if thou shalt hearken diligently unto the voice of the Lord thy God, to observe and to do all his commandments which I command thee this day, that the Lord thy God will set thee on high above all nations of the earth: And all these blessings shall come on thee, and overtake thee, if thou shalt hearken unto the voice of the Lord thy God.

Blessed shalt thou be in the city, and blessed shalt thou be in the field. Blessed shall be the fruit of thy body, and the fruit of thy ground, and the fruit of thy cattle, the increase of thy kine, and the flocks of thy sheep. Blessed shall be thy basket and thy store. Blessed shalt thou be when thou comest in, and blessed shalt thou be when thou goest out.

The Lord shall cause thine enemies that rise up against thee to be smitten before thy face: they shall come out against thee one way, and flee before thee seven ways. The Lord shall command the blessing upon thee in thy storehouses, and in all that thou settest thine hand unto; and he shall bless thee in the land which the Lord thy God giveth thee.

The Lord shall establish thee an holy people unto himself, as he hath sworn unto thee, if thou shalt keep the commandments of the Lord thy God, and walk in his ways. And all people of the earth shall see that thou art called by the name of the Lord; and they shall be afraid of thee.

And the Lord shall make thee plenteous in goods, in the fruit of thy body, and in the fruit of thy cattle, and in the fruit of thy ground, in the land which the Lord sware unto thy fathers to give thee. The Lord shall open unto thee his good treasure, the heaven to give the rain unto thy land in his season, and to bless all the work of thine hand: and thou shalt lend unto many nations, and thou shalt not borrow.

And the Lord shall make thee the head, and not the tail; and thou shalt be above only, and thou shalt not be beneath; if that thou hearken unto the commandments of the Lord thy God, which I command thee this day, to observe and to do them: And thou shalt not go aside from any of the words which I command thee this day, to the right hand, or to the left, to go after other gods to serve them.

Amp—If you will listen diligently to the voice of the Lord your God, being watchful to do all His commandments which I command you this day, the Lord your God will set you high above all the nations of the earth, And all these blessings shall come upon you and overtake you, if you heed the voice of the Lord your God.

Blessed shall you be in the city, and blessed shall you be in the field. Blessed shall be the fruit of your body, and the fruit of your ground, and the fruit of your beasts, the increase of your cattle, and the young of your flock. Blessed shall be your basket and your kneading trough. Blessed shall you be when you come in, and blessed shall you be when you go out.

The Lord shall cause your enemies who rise up against you to be defeated before your face; they shall come out against you one way, and flee before you seven ways. The Lord shall command the blessing upon you in your storehouse, and in all that you undertake; and He will bless you in the land which the Lord your God gives you.

The Lord will establish you as a people holy to Himself, as He has sworn to you, if you keep the commandments of the Lord your God, and walk in His ways. And all people of the earth shall see that you are called by the name [and in the presence of] the Lord; and they shall be afraid of you.

And the Lord shall make you have a surplus of prosperity, through the fruit of your body, of your livestock, and of your ground, in the land which the Lord swore to your fathers to give you. The Lord shall open to you His good treasury, the heavens to give the rain of your land in its season, and to bless all the work of your hand; and you shall lend to many nations, but you shall not borrow.

And the Lord shall make you the head, and not the tail; and you shall be above only, and you shall not be beneath, if you heed the commandments of the Lord your God, which I command you this day, and are watchful to do them. And you shall not go aside from any of the words which I command you this day, to the right hand or to the left, to go after other gods to serve them.

Moffatt—If only you will listen carefully to what the Eternal your God orders, mindful to carry out all his commands which I enjoin upon you this day, then the Eternal your God will lift you high above all the nations of the earth, and all these blessings shall come upon you and overtake you, if only you listen to the voice of the Eternal your God.

You shall be blessed in town and in country; blessed shall be the fruit of your body and of your ground, the young of your cattle and the lambs of your flock; full shall your basket be, and your kneading-trough; blessed shall you be as you start out and as you come home.

*Prosperity
Is a Covenant
Blessing*

The foes who attack you the Eternal will rout before you; they may assail you all together, but they shall fly before you in all directions. The Eternal will command you to be blessed in your barns and in every enterprise to which you put your hand, blessing you in the land which the Eternal your God assigns to you.

The Eternal will confirm your position as a people sacred to himself, as he swore to you, if you obey the orders of the Eternal your God and live his life, so that when all nations on earth see you are owned by the Eternal, they may stand in awe of you.

The Eternal will make you overflow with prosperity in the fruit of your body, of your cattle, and of your ground, the ground that the Eternal swore to your fathers that he would give you. The Eternal will open his rich treasury of heaven for you, to bestow rain in due season on your land, blessing all your labours, so that you shall lend to many a nation but never need to borrow from them.

So shall the Eternal put you at the head, not at the tail; you shall be always rising, never falling, as you listen to the commands of the Eternal your God which I enjoin upon you this day, and carry them out carefully, never swerving to right or to left from any of the injunctions I lay upon you this day, by going after any other gods to worship them.

NIV—If you fully obey the Lord your God and carefully follow all his commands I give you today, the Lord your God will set you high above all the nations on earth. All these blessings will come upon you and accompany you if you obey the Lord your God:

You will be blessed in the city and blessed in the country. The fruit of your womb will be blessed, and the crops of your land and the young of your livestock—the calves of your herds and the lambs of your flocks. Your basket and your kneading trough will be blessed. You will be blessed when you come in and blessed when you go out.

The Lord will grant that the enemies who rise up against you will be defeated before you. They will come at you from one direction but flee from you in seven. The Lord will send a blessing on your barns and on everything you put your hand to. The Lord your God will bless you in the land he is giving you.

The Lord will establish you as his holy people, as he promised you on oath, if you keep the commands of the Lord your God and walk in his ways. Then all the peoples on earth will see that you are called by the name of the Lord, and they will fear you.

The Lord will grant you abundant prosperity—in the fruit of your womb, the young of your livestock and the crops of your ground—in the land he swore to your forefathers to give you. The Lord will open the heavens, the storehouse of his bounty, to send rain on your land in season and to bless all the work of your hands. You will lend to many nations but will borrow from none.

Prosperity
Is a Covenant
Blessing

The Lord will make you the head, not the tail. If you pay attention to the commands of the Lord your God that I give you this day and carefully follow them, you will always be at the top, never at the bottom. Do not turn aside from any of the commands I give you today, to the right or to the left, following other gods and serving them.

Deuteronomy 29:9

KJV—Keep therefore the words of this covenant, and do them, that ye may prosper in all that ye do.

Amp—Therefore keep the words of this covenant, and do them, that you may deal wisely and prosper in all that you do.

Moffatt—Keep the terms of this compact, then, obey them, that you may succeed in all you undertake.

NIV—Carefully follow the terms of this covenant, so that you may prosper in everything you do.

Deuteronomy 30:15-16

KJV—See, I have set before thee this day life and good, and death and evil; In that I command thee this day to love the Lord thy God, to walk in his ways, and to keep his commandments and his statutes and his judgments, that thou mayest live and multiply: and the Lord thy God shall bless thee in the land whither thou goest to possess it.

Amp—See, I have set before you this day life and good, and death and evil. [If you obey the commandments of the Lord your God which] I command you today, to love the Lord your God, to walk in His ways, and to keep His commandments and His statutes and His ordinances, then you shall live and multiply, and the Lord your God will bless you in the land which you go to possess.

Moffatt—Here have I put before you this day life and welfare, death and misfortune. If you listen to the orders of the Eternal your God which I enjoin upon you this day, to love the Eternal your God, to live his life, to follow his orders and rules and regulations, then you shall live and multiply, and the Eternal your God will bless you in the land which you are entering to occupy.

NIV—See, I set before you today life and prosperity, death and destruction. For I command you today to love the Lord your God, to walk in his ways, and to keep his commands, decrees and laws; then you will live and increase, and the Lord your God will bless you in the land you are entering to possess.

Psalm 111:1-6

KJV—Praise ye the Lord. I will praise the Lord with my whole heart, in the assembly of the upright, and in the congregation. The works of the Lord are great, sought out of all them that have pleasure therein. His work is honourable and glorious: and his righteousness endureth for ever. He hath made his wonderful works to be remembered: the Lord is gracious and full of compassion. He hath given meat unto them that fear him: he will ever be mindful of his covenant. He hath shown his people the power of his works, that he may give them the heritage of the heathen.

Amp—Praise the Lord!—Hallelujah! I will praise and give thanks to the Lord with my whole heart, in the council of the upright, and in the congregation. The works of the Lord are great, sought out by all those who have delight in them. His work is honorable and glorious, and His righteousness endures for ever. He has made His wonderful works to be remembered; the Lord is gracious, merciful and full of loving compassion. He has given food and provision to those who reverently and worshipfully fear Him; He will remember His covenant for ever and imprint it [on His mind]. He has declared and shown to His people the power of His works, in giving them the heritage of the nations [of Canaan].

Moffatt—Hallelujah. With all my heart I thank the Eternal, in gatherings of good men for fellowship. Great are the Eternal's doings, to be studied by all who delight in them; splendid and glorious are his deeds, his victories know no end; he will have us celebrate his wondrous deeds, for the Eternal is gracious and pitiful. He feeds his worshippers; never does he forget his compact. He has shown his people his power in action, as he gave them the homes of the heathen.

NIV—Praise the Lord. I will extol the Lord with all my heart in the council of the upright and in the assembly. Great are the works of the Lord; they are pondered by all who delight in them. Glorious and majestic are his deeds, and his righteousness endures forever. He has caused his wonders to be remembered; the Lord is gracious and compassionate. He provides food for those who fear him; he remembers his covenant forever. He has shown his people the power of his works, giving them the lands of other nations.

Psalm 112:1-9

KJV—Praise ye the Lord. Blessed is the man that feareth the Lord, that delighteth greatly in his commandments. His seed shall be mighty upon earth: the generation of the upright shall be blessed. Wealth and riches shall be in his house: and his righteousness

endureth for ever. Unto the upright there
ariseth light in the darkness: he is gracious,
and full of compassion, and righteous.

A good man showeth favour, and lendeth: he will guide his affairs with discretion.
Surely he shall not be moved for ever: the
righteous shall be in everlasting remembrance. He shall not be afraid of evil tidings:
his heart is fixed, trusting in the Lord. His
heart is established, he shall not be afraid,
until he see his desire upon his enemies. He
hath dispersed, he hath given to the poor;
his righteousness endureth for ever; his
horn shall be exalted with honour.

Amp—Praise the Lord—Hallelujah! Blessed—
happy, fortunate [to be envied]—is the man
who fears (reveres and worships) the Lord,
who delights greatly in His commandments.
His [spiritual] offspring shall be a mighty one
upon earth; the generation of the upright
shall be blessed. Prosperity and welfare are
in his house, and his righteousness endures
for ever. Light arises in the darkness for the
upright, gracious, compassionate and just—
who are in right standing with God.

It is well with the man who deals generously and lends, who conducts his affairs
with justice. He will not be moved, for ever;
the [uncompromisingly] righteous—the upright, in right standing with God—shall be in
everlasting remembrance. He shall not be
afraid of evil tidings; his heart is firmly fixed,

trusting (leaning on and being confident) in the Lord. His heart is established and steady, he will not be afraid while he waits to see his desire upon his adversaries. He has distributed freely, he has given to the poor and needy; his righteousness—uprightness and right standing with God—endures for ever; his horn shall be exalted in honor.

Moffatt—Hallelujah. Happy the man who reverences the Eternal, who finds rich joy in his commands! His children rise to power within the land; the race of the upright are blessed. Riches and wealth are in his house, good fortune never fails him. Light dawns on the good man, the upright man so mild and merciful.

All goes well with the generous, open-handed, who will act fairly, never shall that man come to grief; the good man's memory never fades. He has no fear of evil tidings, he trusts the Eternal with a steady heart; his heart is firm and fearless, certain that he will see his foes collapse. He gives to the poor lavishly, and so good fortune never fails him—he rises to high power and honour.

NIV—Praise the Lord. Blessed is the man who fears the Lord, who finds great delight in his commands. His children will be mighty in the land; the generation of the upright will be blessed. Wealth and riches are in his house, and his righteousness endures forever. Even in darkness light dawns for the upright, for the gracious and compassionate and righteous man.

Good will come to him who is generous and lends freely, who conducts his affairs with justice. Surely he will never be shaken; a righteous man will be remembered forever. He will have no fear of bad news; his heart is steadfast, trusting in the Lord. His heart is secure, he will have no fear; in the end he will look in triumph on his foes. He has scattered abroad his gifts to the poor, his righteousness endures forever; his horn will be lifted high in honor.

Psalm 132:12-18

KJV—If thy children will keep my covenant and my testimony that I shall teach them, their children shall also sit upon thy throne for evermore. For the Lord hath chosen Zion; he hath desired it for his habitation. This is my rest for ever: here will I dwell; for I have desired it. I will abundantly bless her provision: I will satisfy her poor with bread. I will also clothe her priests with salvation: and her saints shall shout aloud for joy. There will I make the horn of David to bud: I have ordained a lamp for mine anointed. His enemies will I clothe with shame: but upon himself shall his crown flourish.

Amp—If your children will keep My covenant and My testimony that I shall teach them, their children also shall sit upon your throne for ever. For the Lord has chosen Zion; He has desired it for His habitation. This is My resting place for ever [says the Lord]; here will I dwell, for I have desired it. I will surely and abundantly bless her provision; I will satisfy her poor with bread. Her priests also will I clothe with salvation, and her saints shall shout aloud for joy. There will I make a horn spring forth unto David and bud; I have ordained and prepared a lamp for My anointed [fulfilling the promises of old]. His enemies will I clothe with shame, but upon himself shall his crown flourish.

Moffatt—"If your sons will keep my compact and the laws I teach them, their sons shall also sit for ever on your throne." For the Eternal has chosen Sion as the seat that he desires; "Here is my resting-place," he says, "the seat I choose for evermore; I will enrich her food-supplies, and satisfy her poor with bread. I will robe her priests in triumph, and make her worshippers shout for joy. There will I make David's dynasty flourish, and my chosen king shine prosperously; his foes I shroud with dark disgrace, but his own crown shall sparkle."

NIV—"If your sons keep my covenant and the statutes I teach them, then their sons will

*Prosperity
Is a Covenant
Blessing*

sit on your throne for ever and ever." For the Lord has chosen Zion, he has desired it for his dwelling: "This is my resting place for ever and ever; here I will sit enthroned, for I have desired it—I will bless her with abundant provisions; her poor will I satisfy with food. I will clothe her priests with salvation, and her saints will ever sing for joy. Here I will make a horn grow for David and set up a lamp for my anointed one. I will clothe his enemies with shame, but the crown on his head will be resplendent."

Zechariah 8:12

KJV—For the seed shall be prosperous; the vine shall give her fruit, and the ground shall give her increase, and the heavens shall give their dew; and I will cause the remnant of this people to possess all these things.

Amp—For there shall be the seed sowing of peace and prosperity; the vine shall yield her fruit, and the ground shall give its increase, and the heavens shall give their dew; and I will cause the remnant of this people to inherit and possess all these things.

Moffatt—For I will sow peace and prosperity, the vine shall bear fruit, the ground shall yield its produce, and the skies drop dew—blessings that I will make lasting for those left of my people.

NIV—The seed will grow well, the vine will yield its fruit, the ground will produce its crops, and the heavens will drop their dew. I will give all these things as an inheritance to the remnant of this people.

The old covenant provided many wonderful promises, including prosperity, for God's people. The book of Hebrews tells us that through Jesus, we now have a superior covenant with better promises. And 2 Corinthians 1:19-20 says that in Jesus, all the promises of God are "yes and amen." So the provisions we have under the new covenant are even greater than under the old.

Hebrews 7:19-22

KJV—For the law made nothing perfect, but the bringing in of a better hope did; by the which we draw nigh unto God. And inasmuch as not without an oath he [Jesus] was made priest: (For those priests were made without an oath; but this with an oath by him that said unto him, The Lord sware and will not repent, Thou art a priest for ever after the order of Melchisedec:) By so much was Jesus made a surety of a better testament.

Amp—For the Law never made anything perfect, but instead a better hope is introduced through which we [now] come close to God. And it was not without the taking of an oath [that Christ was made Priest]. For those who formerly became priests received their office without its being confirmed by the taking of an oath by God, but the One was designated and addressed and saluted with an oath, The Lord has sworn and will not regret it or change His mind, You are a Priest forever according to the order of Melchizedek. In keeping with [the oath's greater strength and force], Jesus has become the Guarantee of a better (stronger) agreement—a more excellent and more advantageous covenant.

Moffatt—(For the Law made nothing perfect), and there is introduced a better Hope, by means of which we can draw near to God. A better Hope, because it was not promised apart from an oath. Previous priests became priests apart from any oath, but he [Jesus] has an oath from Him who said to him, The Lord has sworn, and he will not change his mind, thou art a priest for ever. And this makes Jesus surety for a superior covenant.

NIV—(For the law made nothing perfect), and a better hope is introduced, by which we draw near to God. And it was not without an oath! Others became priests without any oath, but he [Jesus] became a priest with an oath when God said to him: "The

Lord has sworn and will not change his mind: 'You are a priest forever.'" Because of this oath, Jesus has become the guarantee of a better covenant.

Hebrews 8:6

KJV—But now hath he [Jesus] obtained a more excellent ministry, by how much also he is the mediator of a better covenant, which was established upon better promises.

Amp—But as it now is, He [Christ] has acquired a [priestly] ministry which is as much superior and more excellent [than the old] as the covenant—the agreement—of which he is the Mediator (the Arbiter, Agent) is superior and more excellent; [because] it is enacted and rests upon more important (sublimer, higher and nobler) promises.

Moffatt—As it is, however, the divine service he [Jesus] has obtained is superior, owing to the fact that he mediates a superior covenant, enacted with superior promises.

NIV—But the ministry Jesus has received is as superior to theirs as the covenant of which he is mediator is superior to the old one, and it is founded on better promises.

Prosperity Is Wisdom, Favor and Success

God wants to bless you so you can *be* a blessing. He'll do that by causing you to grow spiritually in your knowledge of Him and to grow strong in character and full of wisdom by acting on that knowledge. In other words, the more we begin to imitate God's ways in our own actions, the more we put ourselves in position for Him to bless us greatly.

Joseph is a perfect example of that truth (see Genesis 37, 39-45).

Right in the middle of slavery, God gave Joseph such wisdom, ability and favor that he made his slave master rich. As a result, the man put Joseph in charge of all his possessions. Joseph's circumstances looked bad for a while. But the wisdom and favor of God continually brought him success. Finally, Joseph ended up in charge of the entire country. During the time of famine when Joseph was second in command, other nations came to Egypt for food.

Over and over, in the midst of adversity, Joseph's soul prospered. And his prosperity greatly affected other people—within and far beyond the borders of Egypt. Just *one* person walking in wisdom, favor and success from God can bless nations. Much like Joseph, that one person can be you!

Wisdom

Our ability to prosper is based on more than just believing God. There is a part for us to play in our own prosperity, and the Word of God outlines what we must do in order to prosper. We know that we must be givers, but our responsibility doesn't stop there. The Bible shows us that God wants His people to grow up and act as wise adults, making wise choices. According to the Bible, wisdom is the *principal* or *supreme* thing (Proverbs 4:7). If wisdom is the number one thing we should be seeking, then let's study it more closely and see what God says about it.

In Proverbs 3, we are told that wisdom is more precious than rubies, silver or other riches. In fact, verse 14 even says it is better to get wisdom than gold because it *"yields better returns than gold"* (New International Version). For when a person has wisdom and understanding, they can know how to receive the other things they need—benefits such as promotion, honor, length of days and riches, just to name a few.

Having the wisdom to make the right decision every time, based on the understanding you have received from God's Word and the leading of the Holy Spirit, helps you become prosperous in every area of life. No wonder Proverbs 3:13 says, "*Happy is the man that findeth wisdom, and the man that getteth understanding.*"

2 Chronicles 1:12

KJV—Wisdom and knowledge is granted to thee; and I will give thee riches and wealth, and honour, such as none of the kings have had that have been before thee, neither shall there any after thee have the like.

Amp—Wisdom and knowledge are granted you, and I will give you riches, possessions, honor and glory, such as none of the kings had before you, and none after you shall have their equal.

Moffatt—Wisdom and intelligence I give you, and I will add riches, wealth, and honour such as no king before you ever had, and no king after you will ever have.

NIV—Therefore wisdom and knowledge will be given you. And I will also give you wealth, riches and honor, such as no king who was before you ever had and none after you will have.

Proverbs 2:6-7

KJV—For the Lord giveth wisdom: out of his mouth cometh knowledge and under-standing. He layeth up sound wisdom for the righteous: he is a buckler to them that walk uprightly.

Amp—For the Lord gives skillful and godly Wisdom; from His mouth come knowledge and understanding. He hides away sound and godly Wisdom and stores it for the righteous—those who are upright and in right standing with Him; He is a shield to those who walk uprightly and in integrity.

Moffatt—For it is the Eternal who supplies wisdom, from him come insight and knowl-edge, he has help ready for the upright, he is a shield for those who live honestly.

NIV—For the Lord gives wisdom, and from his mouth come knowledge and understanding. He holds victory in store for the upright, he is a shield to those whose walk is blameless.

Proverbs 3:13-18

KJV—Happy is the man that findeth wisdom, and the man that getteth understanding. For the merchandise of it is better than the merchandise of silver, and the gain thereof than fine gold. She is more precious than rubies: and all the things thou canst desire are not to be compared unto her. Length of days is in her right hand; and in her left hand riches and honour. Her ways are ways of pleasantness, and all her paths are peace. She is a tree of life to them that lay hold upon her: and happy is every one that retaineth her.

Amp—Happy—blessed, fortunate [enviable]—is the man who finds skillful and godly Wisdom, and the man who gets understanding—drawing it forth [from God's Word and life's experiences]. For the gaining of it is better than the gaining of silver, and the profit of it than fine gold. Skillful and godly Wisdom is more precious than rubies, and nothing you can wish for is to be compared to her. Length of days is in her right hand, and in her left hand are riches and honor. Her ways are highways of pleasantness, and all her paths are peace. She is a tree of life to those who lay hold on her, and happy—blessed, fortunate [to be envied]—is every one who holds her fast.

Prosperity Is Wisdom, Favor and Success

Moffatt—Happy is the man who gathers wisdom, the man who gains knowledge: her profits are richer than silver, she brings in more than gold; she is more precious than rubies, no treasure can compare with her; long days lie in her right hand, wealth and honour in her left; her ways are ways of tranquil ease, and all her paths are bliss: to those who grasp her, she is vital strength— happy are all who hold her fast.

Prosperity Promises

NIV—Blessed is the man who finds wisdom, the man who gains understanding, for she is more profitable than silver and yields better returns than gold. She is more precious than rubies; nothing you desire can compare with her. Long life is in her right hand; in her left hand are riches and honor. Her ways are pleasant ways, and all her paths are peace. She is a tree of life to those who embrace her; those who lay hold of her will be blessed.

Proverbs 4:7-9

KJV—Wisdom is the principal thing; therefore get wisdom: and with all thy getting get understanding. Exalt her, and she shall promote thee: she shall bring thee to honour, when thou dost embrace her. She shall give to thine head an ornament of grace: a crown of glory shall she deliver to thee.

Amp—The beginning of Wisdom is, get Wisdom—skillful and godly Wisdom! For skillful and godly Wisdom is the principal thing. And with all you have gotten get understanding—discernment, comprehension and interpretation. Prize Wisdom highly and exalt her, and she will exalt and promote you; she will bring you to honor when you embrace her. She shall give to your head a wreath of gracefulness; a crown of beauty and glory will she deliver to you.

Moffatt—At any cost get knowledge—never leave her, and she will guard you, love her, and she will take care of you, prize her, and she will promote you, and bring you to honour, if you will embrace her, she will adorn you with charm and crown you with glory.

NIV—Wisdom is supreme; therefore get wisdom. Though it cost all you have, get understanding. Esteem her, and she will exalt you; embrace her, and she will honor you. She will set a garland of grace on your head and present you with a crown of splendor.

Proverbs 16:16

KJV—How much better is it to get wisdom than gold! and to get understanding rather to be chosen than silver!

Amp—How much better it is to get skillful and godly Wisdom than gold! And to get understanding is to be chosen rather than silver.

Moffatt—Better get wisdom than gold, better choose knowledge than silver.

NIV—How much better to get wisdom than gold, to choose understanding rather than silver!

Proverbs 24:14

KJV—So shall the knowledge of wisdom be unto thy soul: when thou hast found it, then there shall be a reward, and thy expectation shall not be cut off.

Amp—So shall you know skillful and godly Wisdom to be your life; if you find it, then shall there be a future and a reward, and your hope and expectation shall not be cut off.

NIV—Know also that wisdom is sweet to your soul; if you find it, there is a future hope for you, and your hope will not be cut off.

Ecclesiastes 2:26

KJV—For God giveth to a man that is good in his sight wisdom, and knowledge, and joy: but to the sinner he giveth travail, to gather and to heap up, that he may give to him that is good before God.

Amp—For to the person who pleases Him God gives wisdom and knowledge and joy; but to the sinner He gives the work of gathering and heaping up, that he may give to one who pleases God.

Moffatt—To a man whom God approves, he grants wisdom, knowledge, and happiness, but he sets a sinner the task of gathering and amassing wealth, only to leave it to the man whom God approves.

NIV—To the man who pleases him, God gives wisdom, knowledge and happiness, but to the sinner he gives the task of gathering and storing up wealth to hand it over to the one who pleases God.

Luke 21:15

KJV—For I will give you a mouth and wisdom, which all your adversaries shall not be able to gainsay nor resist.

Amp—For I [Myself] will give you a mouth and such utterance and wisdom as all of your foes combined will be unable to stand against or refute.

*Prosperity Is
Wisdom, Favor
and Success*

Moffatt—For I will give you words and wisdom that not one of your opponents will be able to meet or refute.

NIV—For I will give you words and wisdom that none of your adversaries will be able to resist or contradict.

1 Corinthians 1:30

KJV—Of him [God] are ye in Christ Jesus, who of God is made unto us wisdom, and righteousness, and sanctification, and redemption.

Amp—It is from Him [God] that you have your life in Christ Jesus, Whom God made our Wisdom from God, [that is, revealed to us a knowledge of the divine plan of salvation previously hidden, manifesting itself as] our Righteousness and thus making us upright and putting us in right standing with God; and our Consecration—making us pure and holy; and our Redemption—providing our ransom from eternal penalty for sin.

Moffatt—This is the God to whom you owe your being in Christ Jesus, whom God has made our "Wisdom," that is, our righteousness and consecration and redemption.

NIV—It is because of him [God] that you are in Christ Jesus, who has become for us

wisdom from God—that is, our righteousness, holiness and redemption.

Colossians 1:9-10

KJV—For this cause we also, since the day
we heard it, do not cease to pray for you,
and to desire that ye might be filled with
the knowledge of his will in all wisdom and
spiritual understanding; That ye might walk
worthy of the Lord unto all pleasing, being
fruitful in every good work, and increasing
in the knowledge of God.

Amp—For this reason, we also, from the
day we heard of it, have not ceased to
pray and make [special] request for you,
[asking] that you may be filled with the full
(deep and clear) knowledge of His will in all
spiritual wisdom [that is, in comprehensive
insight into the ways and purposes of God]
and in understanding and discernment of
spiritual things. That you may walk (live and
conduct yourselves) in a manner worthy of
the Lord, fully pleasing to Him and desiring
to please Him in all things, bearing fruit in
every good work and steadily growing and
increasing in (and by) the knowledge of
God—with fuller, deeper and clearer insight,
acquaintance and recognition.

Moffatt—Hence, from the day we heard of
it, we have never ceased to pray for you,

asking God to fill you with the knowledge of his will in all spiritual wisdom and insight, so that you may lead a life that is worthy of the Lord and give him entire satisfaction. May you be fruitful and increase in the doing of all good, as you thus know God!

NIV—For this reason, since the day we heard about you, we have not stopped praying for you and asking God to fill you with the knowledge of his will through all spiritual wisdom and understanding. And we pray this in order that you may live a life worthy of the Lord and may please him in every way: bearing fruit in every good work, growing in the knowledge of God.

Colossians 2:2-3

KJV—That their hearts might be comforted, being knit together in love, and unto all riches of the full assurance of understanding, to the acknowledgement of the mystery of God, and of the Father, and of Christ; In whom are hid all the treasures of wisdom and knowledge.

Amp—[For my concern is] that their hearts may be braced (comforted, cheered and encouraged) as they are knit together in love, that they may come to have all the abounding wealth and blessings of assured conviction of understanding, and that they may become progressively more intimately acquainted with, and may know more definitely and accurately and thoroughly, that mystic secret of God [which is] Christ, the Anointed One.

In Him all the treasures of [divine] wisdom, [of comprehensive insight into the ways and purposes of God], and [all the riches of spiritual] knowledge and enlightenment are stored up and lie hidden.

Moffatt—May their hearts be encouraged! May they learn the meaning of love! May they have all the wealth of conviction that comes from insight! May they learn to know that open secret of God, the Father of Christ, in whom all the treasures of wisdom and knowledge lie hidden!

NIV—My purpose is that they may be encouraged in heart and united in love, so that they may have the full riches of complete understanding, in order that they may know the mystery of God, namely, Christ, in whom are hidden all the treasures of wisdom and knowledge.

James 1:5

KJV—If any of you lack wisdom, let him ask of God, that giveth to all men liberally, and upbraideth not; and it shall be given him.

Amp—If any of you is deficient in wisdom, let him ask of the giving God [Who gives] to every one liberally and ungrudgingly, without reproaching or faultfinding, and it will be given him.

Moffatt—Whoever of you is defective in wisdom, let him ask God who gives to all men without question or reproach, and the gift will be his.

NIV—If any of you lacks wisdom, he should ask God, who gives generously to all without finding fault, and it will be given to him.

James 3:17

KJV—The wisdom that is from above is first pure, then peaceable, gentle, and easy to be intreated, full of mercy and good fruits, without partiality, and without hypocrisy.

Amp—The wisdom from above is first of all pure (undefiled); then it is peace-loving, courteous (considerate, gentle). [It is willing to] yield to reason, full of compassion and good fruits; it is wholehearted and straightforward, impartial and unfeigned—free from doubts, wavering and insincerity.

Moffatt—The wisdom from above is first of all pure, then peaceable, forbearing, conciliatory, full of mercy and wholesome fruit, unambiguous, straightforward.

NIV—The wisdom that comes from heaven is first of all pure; then peace-loving, considerate, submissive, full of mercy and good fruit, impartial and sincere.

Favor

Prosperity encompasses many good things, including favor. When you have favor, it opens doors for you and causes things to go your way—even when, in the natural, it may not seem possible.

Webster's Dictionary defines favor as "friendly or kind regard, good will, approval, unfair partiality or favoritism." That is what we, as children of God, receive from our Father God. He does show us favoritism, because we're His kids. When we are obedient to do what His Word says and also stand on the promises found there, He can cause people to show us favor.

Proverbs 12:2 says that a good man finds favor with God. If we walk in love, mercy, kindness and truth, we will find favor with God and man (Proverbs 3:1-6).

We should seek the approval and favor of God, not man, because "*if God be for us, who can be against us?*" (Romans 8:31). God will make a covering over and defend those who put their trust in Him. He surrounds them with a shield of favor (Psalm 5:11-12). And He "*is able to make all grace (every favor and earthly blessing)*" come to us in abundance (2 Corinthians 9:8-11). When we have favor with God, people just can't help but help us.

Genesis 39:2-4

KJV—The Lord was with Joseph, and he was a prosperous man; and he was in the house of his master the Egyptian. And his master saw that the Lord was with him, and that the Lord made all that he did to prosper in his hand. And Joseph found grace in his sight.

Amp—The Lord was with Joseph, and he [though a slave] was a successful and prosperous man; and he was in the house of his master the Egyptian. And his master saw that the Lord was with him, and that the Lord made all that he did to flourish and succeed in his hand. So Joseph pleased [Potiphar] and found favor in his sight.

Moffatt—The Eternal was with Joseph, and he prospered; he was kept inside the household of his master the Egyptian, and his master noticed that the Eternal was with him, and that the Eternal prospered everything he took in hand. Joseph was popular with him.

NIV—The Lord was with Joseph and he prospered, and he lived in the house of his Egyptian master. When his master saw that the Lord was with him and that the Lord gave him success in everything he did, Joseph found favor in his eyes.

Genesis 39:21-23

KJV—The Lord was with Joseph, and showed him mercy, and gave him favour in the sight of the keeper of the prison. And the keeper of the prison committed to Joseph's hand all the prisoners that were in the prison; and whatsoever they did there, he was the doer of it. The keeper of the prison looked not to any thing that was under his hand; because the Lord was with him, and that which he did, the Lord made it to prosper.

Amp—The Lord was with Joseph, and showed him mercy and loving-kindness and gave him favor in the sight of the warden of the prison. And the warden of the prison committed to Joseph's care all the prisoners who were in the prison; and whatsoever was done there, he was in charge of it. The prison warden paid no attention to anything that was in [Joseph's] charge, for the Lord was with him and made whatever he did to prosper.

Prosperity Is Wisdom, Favor and Success

Moffatt—In gaol he lay. Yet the Eternal was with Joseph and was kind to him, making him popular with the gaoler, who put Joseph in charge of all the prisoners in the gaol, holding him responsible for anything they did; and the gaoler did not need to attend to anything that Joseph undertook, for the Eternal was with him, and whatever he did the Eternal made it prosper.

NIV—The Lord was with him [Joseph]; he showed him kindness and granted him favor in the eyes of the prison warden. So the warden put Joseph in charge of all those held in the prison, and he was made responsible for all that was done there. The warden paid no attention to anything under Joseph's care, because the Lord was with Joseph and gave him success in whatever he did.

Esther 2:15

KJV—Now when the turn of Esther, the daughter of Abihail the uncle of Mordecai, who had taken her for his daughter, was come to go in unto the king, she required nothing but what Hegai the king's chamberlain, the keeper of the women, appointed. And Esther obtained favour in the sight of all them that looked upon her.

Amp—Now when the turn for Esther the daughter of Abihail, the uncle of Mordecai who had taken her as his own daughter, had come to go in to the king, she required nothing but what Hegai the king's attendant, the keeper of the women, suggested. And Esther won favor in the sight of all who saw her.

Moffatt—When the turn came for Esther, the daughter of Abîhaîl, the uncle of Mordecai (who had adopted her as his daughter), to go to the king, she asked for nothing except what Hegê the king's eunuch advised. Ester won the admiration of all who saw her.

NIV—When the turn came for Esther (the girl Mordecai had adopted, the daughter of his uncle Abihail) to go to the king, she asked for nothing other than what Hegai, the king's eunuch who was in charge of the harem, suggested. And Esther won the favor of everyone who saw her.

Psalm 5:11-12

KJV—But let all those that put their trust in thee rejoice: let them ever shout for joy, because thou defendest them: let them also that love thy name be joyful in thee. For thou, Lord, wilt bless the righteous; with favour wilt thou compass him as with a shield.

Amp—But let all those who take refuge and put their trust in You rejoice; let them ever sing and shout for joy, because You make a covering over them and defend them; let those also who love Your name be joyful in You and be in high spirits. For You, Lord, will bless the [uncompromisingly] righteous [him who is upright and in right standing with You]; as with a shield You will surround him with good will (pleasure and favor).

Moffatt—So all who shelter with thee shall rejoice, and under thy protection sing for joy; lovers of thy name ever exult in thee. For thou wilt bless the just, O thou Eternal, shielding them safe, crowning them with thy favour.

NIV—But let all who take refuge in you be glad; let them ever sing for joy. Spread your protection over them, that those who love your name may rejoice in you. For surely, O Lord, you bless the righteous; you surround them with your favor as with a shield.

Psalm 30:4-5

KJV—Sing unto the Lord, O ye saints of his, and give thanks at the remembrance of his holiness. For his anger endureth but a moment; in his favour is life.

Amp—Sing to the Lord, O you saints of His, and give thanks at the remembrance of His holy name. For His anger is but for a moment, but His favor is for a lifetime or in His favor is life.

Moffatt—Sing praise to the Eternal, ye devout, give thanks, as you recall his sacred name; for his anger only lasts a moment, his favour lasts a lifetime.

NIV—Sing to the Lord, you saints of his; praise his holy name. For his anger lasts only a moment, but his favor lasts a lifetime.

Proverbs 3:1-6

KJV—My son, forget not my law; but let thine heart keep my commandments: For length of days, and long life, and peace, shall they add to thee. Let not mercy and truth forsake thee: bind them about thy neck; write them upon the table of thine heart: So shalt thou find favour and good understanding in the sight of God and man.

Trust in the Lord with all thine heart; and lean not unto thine own understanding. In all thy ways acknowledge him, and he shall direct thy paths.

Prosperity Is Wisdom, Favor and Success

Amp—My son, forget not my law or teaching, but let your heart keep my commandments; For length of days, and years of life [worth living], and tranquility [inward and outward and continuing through old age till death], these shall they add to you. Let not mercy and kindness [shutting out all hatred and selfishness], and truth [shutting out all deliberate hypocrisy or falsehood] forsake you. Bind them about your neck; write them upon the tablet of your heart; So shall you find favor, good understanding and high esteem in the sight [or judgment] of God and man.

Lean on, trust and be confident in the Lord with all your heart and mind, and do not rely on your own insight or understanding. In all your ways know, recognize and acknowledge Him, and He will direct and make straight and plain your paths.

Moffatt—My son, forget not my directions, keep in mind what I command; for that will bring you welfare, long days and happy life. Never let kindness and loyalty go, tie them fast round your neck; so you shall have goodwill and good repute with God and man alike.

Rely with all your heart on the Eternal, and never lean on your own insight; have mind of him wherever you may go, and he will clear the road for you.

NIV—My son, do not forget my teaching, but keep my commands in your heart, for they will prolong your life many years and bring you prosperity. Let love and faithfulness never leave you; bind them around your neck, write them on the tablet of your heart. Then you will win favor and a good name in the sight of God and man.

Trust in the Lord with all your heart and lean not on your own understanding; in all your ways acknowledge him, and he will make your paths straight.

Proverbs 11:27

KJV—He that diligently seeketh good procureth favour: but he that seeketh mischief, it shall come unto him.

Amp—He who diligently seeks good seeks [God's] favor, but he who searches after evil, it shall come upon him.

Moffatt—He whose aims are good wins the goodwill of God: he whose aims are evil, evil shall befall him.

NIV—He who seeks good finds goodwill, but evil comes to him who searches for it.

Proverbs 12:2

KJV—A good man obtaineth favour of the Lord: but a man of wicked devices will he condemn.

Amp—A good man obtains favor of the Lord, but a man of wicked devices He condemns.

Moffatt—A good-natured man has the goodwill of the Eternal, but He passes sentence on malicious men.

NIV—A good man obtains favor from the Lord, but the Lord condemns a crafty man.

Daniel 1:8-9

KJV—Daniel purposed in his heart that he would not defile himself with the portion of the king's meat, nor with the wine which he drank: therefore he requested of the prince of the eunuchs that he might not defile himself. Now God had brought Daniel into favour and tender love with the prince of the eunuchs.

Amp—Daniel determined in his heart that he would not defile himself by [eating his portion of] the king's rich and dainty food or with the wine which he drank; therefore he requested of the chief of the eunuchs that he might be allowed not to defile himself.

Now God made Daniel to find favor, compassion and loving-kindness with the chief of the eunuchs.

Moffatt—Daniel, however, did not intend to be contaminated with the king's food or with the wine he drank; so he asked the governor of the eunuchs that he might not contaminate himself. Now God had made Daniel win favour and pity from the governor of the eunuchs.

NIV—Daniel resolved not to defile himself with the royal food and wine, and he asked the chief official for permission not to defile himself this way. Now God had caused the official to show favor and sympathy to Daniel.

Romans 8:31

KJV—If God be for us, who can be against us?

Amp—If God be for us, who [can be] against us?—Who can be our foe, if God is on our side?

NIV—If God is for us, who can be against us?

2 Corinthians 9:8-11

KJV—God is able to make all grace abound toward you; that ye, always having all sufficiency in all things, may abound to every good work: (As it is written, He hath dispersed abroad; he hath given to the poor: his righteousness remaineth for ever.

Now he that ministereth seed to the sower both minister bread for your food, and multiply your seed sown, and increase the fruits of your righteousness;) Being enriched in every thing to all bountifulness, which causeth through us thanksgiving to God.

Amp—God is able to make all grace (every favor and earthly blessing) come to you in abundance, so that you may always and under all circumstances and whatever the need, be self-sufficient—possessing enough to require no aid or support and furnished in abundance for every good work and charitable donation. As it is written, He [the benevolent person] scatters abroad, He gives to the poor; His deeds of justice and goodness and kindness and benevolence will go on and endure forever!

And [God] Who provides seed for the sower and bread for eating will also provide and multiply your [resources for] sowing, and increase the fruits of your righteousness [which manifests itself in active goodness, kindness and charity]. Thus you will be enriched in all things and in every way, so that you can be generous, [and your generosity as it is] administered by us will bring forth thanksgiving to God.

Moffatt—God is able to bless you with ample means, so that you may always have quite enough for any emergency of your own and ample besides for any kind act to others; as it is written, He scatters his gifts to the poor broadcast, his charity lasts for ever.

He who furnishes the sower with seed and with bread to eat will supply seed for you and multiply it; he will increase the crop of your charities—you will be enriched on all hands, so that you can be generous on all occasions, and your generosity, of which I am the agent, will make men give thanks to God.

Prosperity Is Wisdom, Favor and Success

NIV—God is able to make all grace abound to you, so that in all things at all times, having all that you need, you will abound in every good work. As it is written: "He has scattered abroad his gifts to the poor; his righteousness endures forever."

Now he who supplies seed to the sower and bread for food will also supply and increase your store of seed and will enlarge the harvest of your righteousness. You will be made rich in every way so that you can be generous on every occasion, and through us your generosity will result in thanksgiving to God.

Success

When you succeed at something, you prosper. And the Word of God is our foundation for success in every area of life, including prosperity. As we discussed earlier, God told Joshua to speak, meditate and obey the Word in order to have success. And that is still true for us today. Over and over again, the Scriptures tell us that our focus should be on the Word. It contains God's instructions to us, as well as the promises He has given us to stand on. The answers, and the wisdom to find answers, are in God's Word.

When we are obedient and we please the Lord, He will give us success. He is the One Who teaches us to profit and leads us by the way we should go (Isaiah 48:17).

Have you ever noticed that the Scriptures don't say God will give you just enough to get by? Instead, the Bible uses words like overflow, plentiful and abundance. All God's thoughts are higher than our thoughts and His ways are higher than ours, which explains why Ephesians 3:19-21 says He is able to do exceeding abundantly above all that we ask or think. And what is He thinking regarding us? Jeremiah 29:11 tells us, "For I *know the plans I have for you*," declares the Lord, "*plans to prosper you and not to harm you, plans to give you hope and a future.*" He is planning for us to succeed!

Joshua 1:5, 7-8

KJV—There shall not any man be able to stand before thee all the days of thy life: as I was with Moses, so I will be with thee: I will not fail thee, nor forsake thee....

Only be thou strong and very courageous, that thou mayest observe to do according to all the law, which Moses my servant commanded thee: turn not from it to the right hand or to the left, that thou mayest prosper whithersoever thou goest. This book of the law shall not depart out of thy mouth; but thou shalt meditate therein day and night, that thou mayest observe to do according to all that is written therein: for then thou shalt make thy way prosperous, and then thou shalt have good success.

Amp—No man shall be able to stand before you all the days of your life. As I was with Moses, so I will be with you; I will not fail you or forsake you....

Only you be strong, and very courageous, that you may do according to all the law, which Moses My servant commanded you. Turn not from it to the right hand or to the left, that you may prosper wherever you go. This book of the law shall not depart out of your mouth, but you shall meditate on it day and night, that you may observe and do according to all that is written in it; for then you shall make your

Prosperity Is Wisdom, Favor and Success

way prosperous, and then you shall deal wisely and have good success.

Moffatt—Not a man shall be able to hold his own against you all the days of your life; as I was with Moses, so I will be with you; I will never fail you nor forsake you....

Only be strong and brave, mindful to carry out all your orders from my servant Moses, turning neither to the right nor to the left, so that you may succeed wherever you go. This lawbook you shall never cease to have on your lips; you must pore over it day and night, that you may be mindful to carry out all that is written in it, for so shall you make your way prosperous, so shall you succeed.

NIV—No one will be able to stand up against you all the days of your life. As I was with Moses, so I will be with you; I will never leave you nor forsake you....

Be strong and very courageous. Be careful to obey all the law my servant Moses gave you; do not turn from it to the right or to the left, that you may be successful wherever you go. Do not let this Book of the Law depart from your mouth; meditate on it day and night, so that you may be careful to do everything written in it. Then you will be prosperous and successful.

1 Samuel 2:7-10

KJV—[The Lord] He raiseth up the poor out of the dust, and lifteth up the beggar from the dunghill, to set them among princes, and to make them inherit the throne of glory: for the pillars of the earth are the Lord's, and he hath set the world upon them. He will keep the feet of his saints, and the wicked shall be silent in darkness; for by strength shall no man prevail. The adversaries of the Lord shall be broken to pieces; out of heaven shall he thunder upon them: the Lord shall judge the ends of the earth; and he shall give strength unto his king, and exalt the horn of his anointed.

Amp—[The Lord] He raises up the poor out of the dust, and lifts up the needy from the ash heap, to make them sit with the noble, and inherit the throne of glory. For the pillars of the earth are the Lord's, and He has set the world upon them. He will guard the feet of His godly ones, and the wicked shall be silenced and perish in darkness; for by strength shall no man prevail. The adversaries of the Lord shall be broken to pieces; against them will He thunder in Heaven. The Lord will judge [all peoples] to the ends of the earth; and He will give strength to His king, and exalt the power of His Anointed—His Christ.

117

Prosperity Is Wisdom, Favor and Success

Moffatt—[The Eternal] he lifts the poor out of the dust, he raises beggars from the rubbish heap, seating them next to nobles, to give them thrones of splendour. [[For the pillars of the earth belong to the Eternal, and on them he set the world.]] He will guard the steps of his godly folk, but evil men shall perish in the dark (for no man's strength makes him mighty). The Eternal will crush his enemies, the Most High in heaven will shatter them (the Eternal's judgments shall cover the wide world), to add power to his king, to heighten the strength of his anointed one.

Prosperity Promises

NIV—[The Lord] He raises the poor from the dust and lifts the needy from the ash heap; he seats them with princes and has them inherit a throne of honor. For the foundations of the earth are the Lord's; upon them he has set the world. He will guard the feet of his saints, but the wicked will be silenced in darkness. It is not by strength that one prevails; those who oppose the Lord will be shattered. He will thunder against them from heaven; the Lord will judge the ends of the earth. He will give strength to his king and exalt the horn of his anointed.

2 Kings 18:7

KJV—The Lord was with him [Hezekiah]; and he prospered whithersoever he went forth: and he rebelled against the king of Assyria, and served him not.

Amp—The Lord was with Hezekiah; he prospered wherever he went. And he rebelled against the king of Assyria and refused to serve him.

Moffatt—The Eternal was on [Hezekiah's] side; wherever he made an expedition, he succeeded. He rebelled against the king of Assyria and refused to serve him.

NIV—The Lord was with [Hezekiah]; he was successful in whatever he undertook. He rebelled against the king of Assyria and did not serve him.

2 Chronicles 15:7

KJV—Be ye strong therefore, and let not your hands be weak: for your work shall be rewarded.

Amp—Be strong therefore, and let not your hands be weak and slack, for your work shall be rewarded.

Moffatt—But be you strong, relax not your efforts, for your work will be rewarded.

NIV—But as for you, be strong and do not give up, for your work will be rewarded.

KJV—The Lord was with Jehoshaphat, because he walked in the first ways of his father David, and sought not unto Baalim; But sought to the Lord God of his father, and walked in his commandments, and not after the doings of Israel. Therefore the Lord established the kingdom in his hand; and all Judah brought to Jehoshaphat presents; and he had riches and honour in abundance. And his heart was lifted up in the ways of the Lord: moreover he took away the high places and groves out of Judah.

Amp—The Lord was with Jehoshaphat, because he walked in the first ways of his father; he did not seek the Baals, But sought and yearned with all his desire for the Lord the God of his father and walked in His commandments, and not after the ways of Israel. Therefore, the Lord established the kingdom in his hand; and all Judah brought tribute to Jehoshaphat; and he had great riches and honor. His heart was cheered and his courage was high in the ways of the Lord; moreover he took away the high places and the Asherim out of Judah.

Moffatt—The Eternal was with Jehoshaphat, because he took the line taken at first by his father; he resorted not to the Baals but to his father's God, living by his commands, instead of doing as Israel did. Therefore did the Eternal establish the kingdom under his rule; all Judah brought presents to Jehoshaphat, and he had abundant wealth and honour. He made it his ambition to live on the lines of the Eternal, and proceeded to remove the shrines and sacred poles from Judah.

NIV—The Lord was with Jehoshaphat because in his early years he walked in the ways his father David had followed. He did not consult the Baals but sought the God of his father and followed his commands rather than the practices of Israel. The Lord established the kingdom under his control; and all Judah brought gifts to Jehoshaphat, so that he had great wealth and honor. His heart was devoted to the ways of the Lord; furthermore, he removed the high places and the Asherah poles from Judah.

Psalm 18:19-22

KJV—He [the Lord] brought me forth also into a large place; he delivered me, because he delighted in me. The Lord rewarded me according to my righteousness; according to the cleanness of my hands hath he recompensed me. For I have kept the ways of the Lord, and have not wickedly departed from my God. For all his judgments were before me, and I did not put away his statutes from me.

Amp—He [the Lord] brought me forth also into a large place; He was delivering me, because He was pleased with me and delighted in me. The Lord rewarded me according to my righteousness [my conscious integrity and sincerity with Him]; according to the cleanness of my hands has He recompensed me. For I have kept the ways of the Lord, and have not wickedly departed from my God. For all His ordinances were before me, and I put not away His statutes from me.

Moffatt—[The Eternal] sets me free, in a clear space; as he delights in me, he rescues me. The Eternal deals with me as I am upright, he recompenses me for my clean life; for I have kept to the Eternal's road, and never sinned by swerving from my God; his rules are all before my mind, I never set aside his orders.

NIV—He [the Lord] brought me out into a spacious place; he rescued me because he delighted in me. The Lord has dealt with me according to my righteousness; according to the cleanness of my hands he has rewarded me. For I have kept the ways of the Lord; I have not done evil by turning from my God. All his laws are before me; I have not turned away from his decrees.

Psalm 23:6

KJV—Surely goodness and mercy shall follow me all the days of my life.

Amp—Surely or only goodness, mercy and unfailing love shall follow me all the days of my life.

Moffatt—All through my life Goodness and Kindness wait on me.

NIV—Surely goodness and love will follow me all the days of my life.

Psalm 65:4-13

KJV—Blessed is the man whom thou choosest, and causest to approach unto thee, that he may dwell in thy courts: we shall be satisfied with the goodness of thy house, even of thy holy temple.

By terrible things in righteousness wilt thou answer us, O God of our salvation; who art the confidence of all the ends of the earth, and of them that are afar off upon the sea: Which by his strength setteth fast the mountains; being girded with power: Which stilleth the noise of the seas, the noise of their waves, and the tumult of

123

Prosperity Is Wisdom, Favor and Success

the people. They also that dwell in the uttermost parts are afraid at thy tokens: thou makest the outgoings of the morning and evening to rejoice.

Thou visitest the earth, and waterest it: thou greatly enrichest it with the river of God, which is full of water: thou preparest them corn, when thou hast so provided for it. Thou waterest the ridges thereof abundantly: thou settlest the furrows thereof: thou makest it soft with showers: thou blessest the springing thereof.

Thou crownest the year with thy goodness; and thy paths drop fatness. They drop upon the pastures of the wilderness: and the little hills rejoice on every side. The pastures are clothed with flocks; the valleys also are covered over with corn; they shout for joy, they also sing.

Amp—Blessed—happy, fortunate [to be envied]—is the man whom You choose and cause to come near, that he may dwell in Your courts! We shall be satisfied with the goodness of Your house, Your holy temple.

By fearful and glorious things [that terrify the wicked, but make the godly sing praises] do You answer us in righteousness—rightness and justice—O God of our salvation, You Who are the confidence and hope of all the ends of the earth, and of those far off on the seas; Who by Your might have founded the mountains, being girded with power; Who still the roaring of the seas, the roaring of their waves, and the tumult of the peoples; So that those who dwell in the earth's farthest parts are afraid at nature's signs of Your presence; You make the places where morning and evening have birth to shout for joy.

You visit the earth and saturate it with water, You greatly enrich it; the river of God is full of water; You provide them grain when You have so prepared the earth. You water the field's furrows abundantly, You settle the ridges of it, You make the soil soft with showers, blessing the sprouting of its vegetation.

You crown the year with Your bounty and goodness, the tracks of Your chariot wheels drip with fatness. The luxuriant pastures in the uncultivated country drip [with moisture], and the hills gird themselves with joy. The meadows are clothed with flocks, the valleys also are covered with grain, they shout for joy and sing together.

Moffatt—Happy is he whom thus thou choosest to dwell in thy courts, close to thee. Fain would we have our fill of this, thy house, thy sacred shrine—its bliss!

God of our victory, answering our prayers with deeds of dread, so loyally, all ends of the earth come to rely on thee, and distant shores—thou by whose might the mountains are made firm and strongly

*Prosperity Is
Wisdom, Favor
and Success*

fixed, by whom the roaring seas are stilled, and the tumult of nations, till dwellers at the world's far end are awed at the proofs of thy power and lands of sunrise and of sunset sing joyfully of thee.

Thou art good to the earth, giving water, enriching her greatly with rain from brimming streams divine; thou providest the grain by preparing her duly, watering her furrows well, soaking her ridges, softening her with showers, and blessing all her growth.

Thou art crowning the year with thy goodness; rich stores drop where thou passest, the very pastures of the downs o'erflow, the hills wear girdles of joy, the meadows are clothed with flocks, the valleys covered with corn, shouting and singing for joy.

NIV—Blessed are those you choose and bring near to live in your courts! We are filled with the good things of your house, of your holy temple.

You answer us with awesome deeds of righteousness, O God our Savior, the hope of all the ends of the earth and of the farthest seas, who formed the mountains by your power, having armed yourself with strength, who stilled the roaring of the seas, the roaring of their waves, and the turmoil of the nations. Those living far away fear your wonders; where morning dawns and evening fades you call forth songs of joy.

You care for the land and water it; you enrich it abundantly. The streams of God are filled with water to provide the people with grain, for so you have ordained it. You drench its furrows and level its ridges; you soften it with showers and bless its crops.

You crown the year with your bounty, and your carts overflow with abundance. The grasslands of the desert overflow; the hills are clothed with gladness. The meadows are covered with flocks and the valleys are mantled with grain; they shout for joy and sing.

Isaiah 30:23

KJV—Then shall he give the rain of thy seed, that thou shalt sow the ground withal; and bread of the increase of the earth, and it shall be fat and plenteous: in that day shall thy cattle feed in large pastures.

Amp—Then will He give you rain for your seed with which you sow the soil, and bread grain as the produce of the ground, and it will be rich and plentiful. In that day your cattle will feed in large pastures.

NIV—He will also send you rain for the seed you sow in the ground, and the food that comes from the land will be rich and plentiful. In that day your cattle will graze in broad meadows.

Isaiah 45:2-3

KJV—I will go before thee, and make the crooked places straight: I will break in pieces the gates of brass, and cut in sunder the bars of iron: And I will give thee the treasures of darkness, and hidden riches of secret places, that thou mayest know that I, the Lord, which call thee by thy name, am the God of Israel.

Amp—I will go before you and level the mountains—to make the crooked places straight; I will break in pieces the doors of bronze and cut asunder the bars of iron. And I will give you the treasures of darkness and hidden riches of secret places, that you may know that it is I, the Lord, the God of Israel, Who calls you by your name.

Moffatt—I myself will go before you, levelling the mountains, I will shatter doors of bronze, and cut through iron bars; I will give you hidden treasures, secret hoards; for 'tis I the Eternal who call you by name, I the God of Israel.

NIV—I will go before you and will level the mountains; I will break down gates of bronze and cut through bars of iron. I will give you the treasures of darkness, riches stored in secret places, so that you may know that I am the Lord, the God of Israel, who summons you by name.

Isaiah 48:15, 17

KJV—I, even I, have spoken; yea, I have called him: I have brought him, and he shall make his way prosperous....Thus saith the Lord, thy Redeemer, the Holy One of Israel; I am the Lord thy God which teacheth thee to profit, which leadeth thee by the way that thou shouldest go.

Amp—I, even I, have foretold it; yes, I have called him [Cyrus]; I have brought him, and the Lord shall make his way prosperous.... Thus says the Lord, your Redeemer, the Holy One of Israel: I am the Lord your God Who teaches you to profit, Who leads you by the way that you should go.

Moffatt—I foretold it, 'twas I called him, 'twas I brought him, I have prospered him.... This is the word of the Eternal your deliverer, the Majestic One of Israel: I am the Eternal your God, training you for your good, leading you by the right way.

NIV—I, even I, have spoken; yes, I have called him. I will bring him, and he will succeed in his mission....This is what the Lord says—your Redeemer, the Holy One of Israel: "I am the Lord your God, who teaches you what is best for you, who directs you in the way you should go."

Prosperity Is Wisdom, Favor and Success

Jeremiah 33:9

KJV—It [Jerusalem] shall be to me a name of joy, a praise and an honour before all the nations of the earth, which shall hear all the good that I do unto them: and they shall fear and tremble for all the goodness and for all the prosperity that I procure unto it.

Amp—[Jerusalem] shall be to Me a name of joy, a praise and a glory before all the nations of the earth who shall hear of all the good I do for them, and they shall fear and tremble because of all the good and all the peace, prosperity, security and stability I provide for it.

Moffatt—The city [Jerusalem] shall bring me joy and praise and glory, while all nations of the world, when they hear of all the good I am doing her, shall tremble in awe at all the good and the welfare I provide for her.

NIV—Then this city [Jerusalem] will bring me renown, joy, praise and honor before all nations on earth that hear of all the good things I do for it; and they will be in awe and will tremble at the abundant prosperity and peace I provide for it.

Ephesians 3:19-21
(Pray this for yourself.)

KJV—And to know the love of Christ, which passeth knowledge, that ye might be filled with all the fulness of God. Now unto him that is able to do exceeding abundantly above all that we ask or think, according to the power that worketh in us, Unto him be glory in the church by Christ Jesus throughout all ages, world without end. Amen.

Amp—[That you may really come] to know—practically, through experience for yourselves—the love of Christ, which far surpasses mere knowledge (without experience); that you may be filled (through all your being) unto all the fullness of God— [that is] may have the richest measure of the divine Presence, and become a body wholly filled and flooded with God Himself! Now to Him Who, by (in consequence of) the [action of His] power that is at work within us, is able to [carry out His purpose and] do superabundantly, far over and above all that we [dare] ask or think—infinitely beyond our highest prayers, desires, thoughts, hopes or dreams—To Him be glory in the church and in Christ Jesus throughout all generations, for ever and ever. Amen—so be it.

Prosperity Is Wisdom, Favor and Success

Moffatt—By knowing the love of Christ which surpasses all knowledge! May you be filled with the entire fulness of God! Now to him who by the action of his power within us is able to do all, aye far more than we can ever ask or imagine, to him be glory in the church and in Christ Jesus throughout all generations for ever and ever: Amen.

NIV—And to know this love that surpasses knowledge—that you may be filled to the measure of all the fullness of God. Now to him who is able to do immeasurably more than all we ask or imagine, according to his power that is at work within us, to him be glory in the church and in Christ Jesus throughout all generations, for ever and ever! Amen.

Prosperity Promises

Chapter 5

Prosperity Is Provision,
Protection and Well-being

Satan goes to great lengths to convince God's people that poverty, sickness, calamity and trouble are blessings in disguise. It is *his* perversion of God's creation! If the devil can make us accept his attack as "an act of God" in our life—and he does that through unscriptural religious traditions or doubt and unbelief—he can rob us of everything Jesus died to provide for us. And what's even more tragic about that is, if we don't know and have confidence in what God has provided for us, we won't even try to stop the devil from operating against us. Everything that Jesus bore on the cross for us, it is our responsibility to resist. We begin to walk in divine prosperity with a decision to no longer allow Satan to put symptoms of lack on us—in any area of our life.

If our thinking isn't completely in line with God's Word, the devil can con us into accepting his attacks. He'll try to make us believe that sickness, poverty or anything else contrary to God's Word is actually God's will for us to teach us something—or for some other reason. Nothing could be further from the truth of God's Word.

If you're a born-again child of God, Christ has redeemed you from sickness, poverty, lack and all of the curse (see Galatians 3:13). Deuteronomy 28:15-68 describes the curse of the law. Here are some excerpts from those verses that plainly show poverty and lack for what they really are. There's nothing good about them, and they don't belong to anyone in the family of God. Read them and rejoice that you have just the *opposite* of what is listed here.

If you will not obey the voice of the Lord your God, being watchful to do all His commandments and His statutes which I command you this day, then all these curses shall come upon you and overtake you:

Cursed shall you be in the city, and cursed shall you be in the field. Cursed shall be your basket and your kneading trough. Cursed shall be the fruit of your body, of your land, of the increase of your cattle and the young of your sheep.

Cursed shall you be when you come in, and cursed shall you be when you go out....

And you shall grope at noonday, as the blind grope in darkness, and you shall not prosper in your ways; and you shall be only oppressed and robbed continually, and there shall be no one to save you....

You shall build a house, and not live in it; you shall plant a vineyard and not gather its grapes.... A nation which you have not known shall eat up the fruit of your land and of all your labors; and you shall be only oppressed and crushed continually....

You shall carry much seed out into the field, and shall gather little in; for the locust shall consume it.... You shall plant vineyards and dress them, but shall neither drink of the wine nor gather the grapes; for the worm shall eat them.... All your trees and the fruit of your ground shall the locust possess.

He [the stranger] shall lend to you, and you shall not lend to him; he shall be the head, and you shall be the tail.

All these curses shall come upon you and shall pursue you and overtake you, till you are destroyed, because you do not obey the voice of

**the Lord your God, to keep His com-
mandments and His statutes which
He commanded you....**

**Because you did not serve the
Lord your God with joyfulness of
[mind and] heart [in gratitude] for the
abundance of all [with which He had
blessed you], Therefore you shall
serve your enemies...in hunger and
thirst, in nakedness, and in want of
all things (T*he Amplified Bible*).**

Praise God! As a believer, you can claim
your redemption from *every* curse men-
tioned in Deuteronomy 28! *All the blessings of
Abraham belong to you.* God has blessed you
with all things that pertain to life and godliness (2 Peter 1:3). Included in those "all
things" are health, safety, protection, a good
marriage and anything else that affects
your life.

When you receive salvation, many benefits become available to you in addition to
eternal life—benefits for the here and now
as well as for eternity. Salvation denotes
deliverance, preservation and restoration. It
is material and temporal deliverance from
danger and apprehension (fear). You have
been given a pardon with the rights of
protection, liberty, health, soundness and
wholeness through your acceptance of
Jesus, the Anointed One, as Lord of your life.

Provision

Provision is probably the most obvious aspect of prosperity. The Bible illustrates again and again that the Lord provides for His people. And His provision is whatever you need. That can include finances, but it's much more than that. *"My God shall supply all your need according to his riches in glory by Christ Jesus"* (Philippians 4:19). Whatever you need, whether it's finances, healing, peace, harmony in your family, the salvation of loved ones or any other good thing, God can provide it. *"Those who seek the Lord lack no good thing"* (Psalm 34:10).

Some people believe exclusively for finances to buy the things they need. But if you're only expecting finances, you could miss a harvest that has your name on it. Of course, God can supply finances. But He is not *limited* to operating that way. He may decide to bypass the finances and just get the "things" into your hands. He may give you supernatural deals to stretch your finances, so that you pay only a fraction of the cost of an item. Or He may speak to someone to simply give you what you need. Either way, it's no problem for God, and it's a blessing to you. So expect miracles of provision—and be open to receive them however God sends them.

Prosperity Is
Provision,
Protection and
Well-being

Genesis 15:1

KJV—After these things the word of the Lord came unto Abram in a vision, saying, Fear not, Abram: I am thy shield, and thy exceeding great reward.

Amp—After these things the word of the Lord came to Abram in a vision, saying, Fear not, Abram, I am your shield, your abundant compensation, and your reward shall be exceedingly great.

Moffatt—After this the Eternal said to Abram in a vision, "Fear not, Abram, I will shield you. Rich your reward shall be."

NIV—After this, the word of the Lord came to Abram in a vision: "Do not be afraid, Abram. I am your shield, your very great reward."

Deuteronomy 2:7

KJV—For the Lord thy God hath blessed thee in all the works of thy hand: he knoweth thy walking through this great wilderness: these forty years the Lord thy God hath been with thee; thou hast lacked nothing.

Amp—For the Lord your God has blessed you in all the work of your hand; He knows your walking through this great wilderness;

these forty years the Lord your God has been with you; you have lacked nothing.

Moffatt—For the Eternal your God has always blessed your enterprise. Think how his care brought you through this wide desert; the Eternal your God has been with you all these forty years, and never have you been in want.

NIV—The Lord your God has blessed you in all the work of your hands. He has watched over your journey through this vast desert. These forty years the Lord your God has been with you, and you have not lacked anything.

Deuteronomy 8:7-10

KJV—For the Lord thy God bringeth thee into a good land, a land of brooks of water, of fountains and depths that spring out of valleys and hills; A land of wheat, and barley, and vines, and fig trees, and pomegranates; a land of oil olive, and honey; A land wherein thou shalt eat bread without scarceness, thou shalt not lack any thing in it; a land whose stones are iron, and out of whose hills thou mayest dig brass. When thou hast eaten and art full, then thou shalt bless the Lord thy God for the good land which he hath given thee.

Amp—For the Lord your God is bringing you into a good land, a land of brooks of water, of fountains and springs, flowing forth in valleys and hills; A land of wheat and barley, and vines and fig trees and pomegranates, a land of olive trees and honey, A land in which you shall eat food without shortage, and lack nothing in it, a land whose stones are iron, and out of whose hills you can dig copper. When you have eaten and are full, then you shall bless the Lord your God for all the good land which He has given you.

Moffatt—For the Eternal your God is bringing you into a fine country, a country with streams of water, with springs and pools, welling up in valleys and on the hills, a country of wheat and barley, of vines and fig-trees and pomegranates, of olive oil and honey, a country where you can eat and never famish, where you shall lack for nothing, a country whose ore is iron and from whose hills you can dig copper. You shall eat and be satisfied, and you shall bless the Eternal your God for the fine country he has given you.

NIV—For the Lord your God is bringing you into a good land—a land with streams and pools of water, with springs flowing in the valleys and hills; a land with wheat and barley, vines and fig trees, pomegranates, olive oil and honey; a land where bread will not be scarce and you will lack nothing; a land where the rocks are iron and you can dig copper out of the hills. When you have eaten and are satisfied, praise the Lord your God for the good land he has given you.

Deuteronomy 32:13

KJV—He made him ride on the high places of the earth, that he might eat the increase of the fields; and he made him to suck honey out of the rock, and oil out of the flinty rock.

Amp—He made Israel ride on the high places of the earth, and he ate the increase of the field; and He made him to suck honey out of the rock and oil out of the flinty rock.

Moffatt—He made them masters of the highlands, living off the hills, sucking honey from the very crags and oil from flinty rocks.

NIV—He made him ride on the heights of the land and fed him with the fruit of the fields. He nourished him with honey from the rock, and with oil from the flinty crag.

2 Chronicles 29:2, 32:27-29

KJV—He [Hezekiah] did that which was right in the sight of the Lord....

Prosperity Is Provision, Protection and Well-being

And Hezekiah had exceeding much riches and honour: and he made himself treasuries for silver, and for gold, and for precious stones, and for spices, and for shields, and for all manner of pleasant jewels; Storehouses also for the increase òf corn, and wine, and oil; and stalls for all manner of beasts, and cotes for flocks. Moreover, he provided him cities, and possessions of flocks and herds in abundance: for God had given him substance very much.

Amp—He [Hezekiah] did right in the sight of the Lord....

And Hezekiah had very great wealth and honor, and he made himself treasuries for silver, gold, precious stones, spices, shields, and all kinds of attractive vessels; Storehouses also for the increase of grain, vintage fruits, and oil, and stalls for all kinds of cattle, and sheepfolds. Moreover he provided himself cities, and flocks and herds in abundance; for God had given him very great possessions.

Moffatt—He [Hezekiah] did what was right in the eyes of the Eternal....

Hezekiah had enormous wealth and honour; he supplied himself with treasuries to hold silver, gold, jewels, spices, rarities, and all kinds of handsome articles, also stores for the influx of grain, wine, and oil, barns for all kinds of cattle, and pens for sheep; he acquired enormous numbers of flocks and herds, for God gave him rich possessions.

NIV—He [Hezekiah] did what was right in the eyes of the Lord....

Hezekiah had very great riches and honor, and he made treasuries for his silver and gold and for his precious stones, spices, shields and all kinds of valuables. He also made buildings to store the harvest of grain, new wine and oil; and he made stalls for various kinds of cattle, and pens for the flocks. He built villages and acquired great numbers of flocks and herds, for God had given him very great riches.

Psalm 34:10

KJV—They that seek the Lord shall not want any good thing.

Amp—They who seek (inquire of and require) the Lord [by right of their need and on authority of His Word] none of them shall lack any beneficial thing.

Moffatt—Those who turn to the Eternal lack no good.

NIV—Those who seek the Lord lack no good thing.

Philippians 4:19

KJV—My God shall supply all your need according to his riches in glory by Christ Jesus.

Amp—My God will liberally supply (fill to the full) your every need according to His riches in glory in Christ Jesus.

Moffatt—My God will supply all your own needs from his wealth in Glory in Christ Jesus.

NIV—My God will meet all your needs according to his glorious riches in Christ Jesus.

Protection

Protection is a vital part of being prosperous, and it is shown throughout the Bible as a promise to the people of God.

God is a Father. By His very nature, He wants to protect and nurture His children. The Father's tender heart is revealed in many scriptures. For example, Luke 13:34 says, *"How often would I have gathered thy children together, as a hen doth gather her brood under her wings."* And Psalm 91:4 says, *"He shall cover thee with his feathers, and under his wings shalt thou trust."*

In Second Samuel 22:2-3, God is shown as a strong refuge from danger: *"The Lord is my rock, and my fortress, and my deliverer; The God of my rock; in him will I trust: he is my shield, and the horn of my salvation, my high tower, and my refuge, my saviour; thou savest me from violence."* He longs to shield us beneath the shelter of His wings and hide us in Himself. And He can do that as long as we run into Him and not from Him. When we are obedient and we draw near to Him, He can act as a Father to us.

When we dwell beneath the shelter of God's wings, it's the safest place to be. Even Satan himself cannot touch a person who has been surrounded by God's hedge of protection (Job 1:10). With Jesus as our Savior and Lord, we have protection through His shed blood. As we discussed earlier in this chapter, protection and deliverance from danger are some of the benefits included in salvation. So stand on God's promises concerning protection, and "He *shall give his angels charge over thee, to keep thee in all thy ways"* (Psalm 91:11).

1 Chronicles 16:20-27

KJV—When they went from nation to nation, and from one kingdom to another people; He [the Lord] suffered no man to do them wrong: yea, he reproved kings for their sakes, Saying, Touch not mine anointed, and do my prophets no harm.

Sing unto the Lord, all the earth; show forth from day to day his salvation. Declare his glory among the heathen; his marvelous works among all nations. For great is the Lord, and greatly to be praised: he also is to be feared above all gods. For all the gods of the people are idols: but the Lord made the heavens. Glory and honour are in his presence; strength and gladness are in his place.

Amp—When they went from nation to nation, and from kingdom to another people, He allowed no man to do them wrong; yes, He reproved kings for their sakes, Saying, Touch not My anointed, and do My prophets no harm.

Sing to the Lord, all the earth; show forth from day to day His salvation. Declare His glory among the nations, His marvelous works among all peoples. For great is the Lord and greatly to be praised; He also is to be (reverently) feared above all so-called gods. For all the gods of the people are [lifeless] idols, but the Lord made the heavens. Honor and majesty are [found] in His presence; strength and joy are [found] in His sanctuary.

Moffatt—Wandering from one nation to another, and from realm to realm; but he would not let a man oppress them, he would punish kings on their account, saying, "Never touch my chosen, my prophets never harm."

Sing, all the earth, to the Eternal, day after day tell of his saving aid; let the heathen hear his glory, let every nation know the wonders he has done. For great is the

Eternal, loudly to be praised, and to be feared above all gods; for all gods of the nations are mere idols, but the Eternal made the heavens; grandeur and majesty attend him, splendour and joy are in his temple.

NIV—They wandered from nation to nation, from one kingdom to another. He allowed no man to oppress them; for their sake he rebuked kings: "Do not touch my anointed ones; do my prophets no harm."

Sing to the Lord, all the earth; proclaim his salvation day after day. Declare his glory among the nations, his marvelous deeds among all peoples. For great is the Lord and most worthy of praise; he is to be feared above all gods. For all the gods of the nations are idols, but the Lord made the heavens. Splendor and majesty are before him; strength and joy in his dwelling place.

Job 1:10

KJV—Hast not thou made an hedge about him [Job], and about his house, and about all that he hath on every side? thou hast blessed the work of his hands, and his substance is increased in the land.

Amp—Have You not put a hedge about him [Job] and his house and all that he has, on every side? You have conferred prosperity and happiness upon him in the work of his hands, and his possessions have increased in the land.

Moffatt—Have you not hedged him [Job] safely in, his house and all he has? You have prospered him in his business, and his flocks are teeming on the land.

NIV—Have you not put a hedge around him [Job] and his household and everything he has? You have blessed the work of his hands, so that his flocks and herds are spread throughout the land.

Psalm 61:3-4

KJV—For thou hast been a shelter for me, and a strong tower from the enemy. I will abide in thy tabernacle for ever: I will trust in the covert of thy wings.

Amp—For You have been a shelter and a refuge for me, a strong tower against the adversary. I will dwell in Your tabernacle for ever; let me find refuge and trust in the shelter of Your wings.

Moffatt—O thou who art my refuge, a fortress against the foe. Oh to be a guest of thine for ever! oh to be sheltered underneath thy wings!

NIV—For you have been my refuge, a strong tower against the foe. I long to dwell in your tent forever and take refuge in the shelter of your wings.

Psalm 91

KJV—He that dwelleth in the secret place of the most High shall abide under the shadow of the Almighty. I will say of the Lord, He is my refuge and my fortress: my God; in him will I trust. Surely he shall deliver thee from the snare of the fowler, and from the noisome pestilence. He shall cover thee with his feathers, and under his wings shalt thou trust: his truth shall be thy shield and buckler.

Thou shalt not be afraid for the terror by night; nor for the arrow that flieth by day; Nor for the pestilence that walketh in darkness; nor for the destruction that wasteth at noonday. A thousand shall fall at thy side, and ten thousand at thy right hand; but it shall not come nigh thee. Only with thine eyes shalt thou behold and see the reward of the wicked. Because thou hast made the Lord, which is my refuge, even the most High, thy habitation; There shall no evil befall thee, neither shall any plague come nigh thy dwelling.

For he shall give his angels charge over thee, to keep thee in all thy ways. They shall bear thee up in their hands, lest thou

Prosperity Is Provision, Protection and Well-being

dash thy foot against a stone. Thou shalt tread upon the lion and adder: the young lion and the dragon shalt thou trample under feet. Because he hath set his love upon me, therefore will I deliver him: I will set him on high, because he hath known my name. He shall call upon me, and I will answer him: I will be with him in trouble; I will deliver him, and honour him. With long life will I satisfy him, and show him my salvation.

Amp—He who dwells in the secret place of the Most High shall remain stable and fixed under the shadow of the Almighty [Whose power no foe can withstand]. I will say of the Lord, He is my refuge and my fortress, my God, on Him I lean and rely, and in Him I (confidently) trust! For [then] He will deliver you from the snare of the fowler and from the deadly pestilence. [Then] He will cover you with His pinions and under His wings shall you trust and find refuge; His truth and His faithfulness are a shield and a buckler. [Then]

You shall not be afraid of the terror of the night, nor of the arrow [the evil plots and slanders of the wicked] that flies by day, Nor of the pestilence that stalks in darkness, nor of the destruction and sudden death that surprise and lay waste at noonday. [Then] A thousand may fall at your side, and ten thousand at your right hand, but it shall not come near you. Only a spectator shall you be [yourself inaccessible in the secret place of the Most High] as you witness the reward of the wicked. Because you have made the Lord your refuge, and the Most High your dwelling place, There shall no evil befall you, nor any plague or calamity come near your tent.

For He will give His angels [especial] charge over you, to accompany and defend and preserve you in all your ways [of obedience and service]. They shall bear you up on their hands, lest you dash your foot against a stone. You shall tread upon the lion and adder, the young lion and the serpent shall you trample under foot. Because he has set his love upon Me, therefore will I deliver him; I will set him on high, because he knows and understands My name [has a personal knowledge of My mercy, love and kindness; trusts and relies on Me, knowing I will never forsake him, no, never]. He shall call upon Me, and I will answer him; I will be with him in trouble, I will deliver him and honor him. With long life will I satisfy him, and show him My salvation.

Moffatt—Happy the man who stays by the Most High in shelter, who lives under the shadow of Almighty God, who calls the Eternal "My refuge and my fortress, my God in whom I trust"! He saves you from the fowler's snare and from the deadly pit;

he protects you with his pinions and hides you underneath his wings.

You need not fear the terrors of the night, nor arrows flying in the day; you need not fear plague stalking in the dark, nor sudden death at noon; hundreds may fall beside you, thousands at your right hand, but the plague will never reach you, safe shielded by his faithfulness. You have only to look on and see how evil men are punished; but you have sheltered beside the Eternal, and made the Most High God your home, so no scathe can befall you, no plague can approach your tent.

For he puts you under his angels' charge, to guard you wherever you go, to lift you in their hands lest you trip over a stone; you can walk over reptiles and cobras, trampling on lions and on dragons. "He clings to me, so I deliver him; I set him safe, because he cares for me; I will answer his cry and be with him in trouble, delivering him and honouring him; I will satisfy him with long life, and let him see my saving care."

NIV—He who dwells in the shelter of the Most High will rest in the shadow of the Almighty. I will say of the Lord, "He is my refuge and my fortress, my God, in whom I trust." Surely he will save you from the fowler's snare and from the deadly pestilence. He will cover you with his feathers, and under his wings you will find refuge; his faithfulness will be your shield and rampart.

You will not fear the terror of night, nor the arrow that flies by day, nor the pestilence that stalks in the darkness, nor the plague that destroys at midday. A thousand may fall at your side, ten thousand at your right hand, but it will not come near you. You will only observe with your eyes and see the punishment of the wicked. If you make the Most High your dwelling—even the Lord, who is my refuge—then no harm will befall you, no disaster will come near your tent.

For he will command his angels concerning you to guard you in all your ways; they will lift you up in their hands, so that you will not strike your foot against a stone. You will tread upon the lion and the cobra; you will trample the great lion and the serpent. "Because he loves me," says the Lord, "I will rescue him; I will protect him, for he acknowledges my name. He will call upon me, and I will answer him; I will be with him in trouble, I will deliver him and honor him. With long life will I satisfy him and show him my salvation."

Isaiah 54:17

KJV—No weapon that is formed against thee shall prosper; and every tongue that shall rise against thee in judgment thou shalt condemn. This is the heritage of the servants of the Lord, and their righteousness is of me, saith the Lord.

Amp—No weapon that is formed against you shall prosper, and every tongue that shall rise against you in judgment you shall show to be in the wrong. This [peace, righteousness, security, triumph over opposition] is the heritage of the servants of the Lord [those in whom the ideal Servant of the Lord is reproduced]. This is the righteousness or the vindication which they obtain from Me—this is that which I impart to them as their justification—says the Lord.

Moffatt—No weapon forged against you shall succeed, no tongue raised against you shall win its plea. Such is the lot of the Eternal's servants; thus, the Eternal promises, do I maintain their cause.

NIV—"No weapon forged against you will prevail, and you will refute every tongue that accuses you. This is the heritage of the servants of the Lord, and this is their vindication from me," declares the Lord.

Ezekiel 34:27

KJV—The tree of the field shall yield her fruit, and the earth shall yield her increase, and they shall be safe in their land, and shall know that I am the Lord, when I have broken the bands of their yoke, and delivered them out of the hand of those that served themselves of them.

Amp—The tree of the field shall yield its fruit, and the earth shall yield its increase, and [My people] shall be secure in their land; and they shall be confident and know—understand and realize—that I am the Lord, when I have broken the bars of their yoke, and have delivered them out of the hand of those who made slaves of them.

Moffatt—The trees of the field shall bear fruit, the earth shall bring forth crops, and they shall live undisturbed in the land; they shall learn that I am the Eternal, when I break their yoke of slavery and rescue them from those who made them slaves.

NIV—The trees of the field will yield their fruit and the ground will yield its crops; the people will be secure in their land. They will know that I am the Lord, when I break the bars of their yoke and rescue them from the hands of those who enslaved them.

2 Thessalonians 3:3

KJV—The Lord is faithful, who shall stablish you, and keep you from evil.

Amp—The Lord is faithful and He will strengthen [you] and set you on a firm foundation and guard you from the evil [one].

Moffatt—The Lord is faithful; he will be sure to strengthen you and protect you from the Evil one.

NIV—The Lord is faithful, and he will strengthen and protect you from the evil one.

Well-being

Well-being is defined in *Webster's Dictionary* as "the state of being well, happy or prosperous." Truly, all is well in your life when you and your loved ones are healthy, happy and prosperous.

Psalm 35:27 says the Lord "*delights in the well-being of his servant*" (New International Version). And 3 John 2 says, "*I pray that you may prosper in every way and [that your body] may keep well even as [I know] your soul keeps well and prospers*" (The Amplified Bible). The Lord is concerned about our total well-being.

The Scriptures repeatedly tell us that it will be well with those who obey the Lord and do what is right in His sight. Then He is free to bless them in every way.

God doesn't wait for circumstances to be perfect before He blesses His people. Romans 4:17 says He calls "*those things which be not as though they were.*" So our well-being is not tied to circumstances, it is tied to God and His Word. He can create whatever He needs to bless us. He can bless us in the midst of a famine just as easily as when things are in abundance (Genesis 26:1-3). He blessed the children of Israel while they wandered in the wilderness, and He blessed Joseph while he was in captivity. He even blessed Abraham and Sarah with a child when, in the natural, it was impossible—and went on to make Abraham the "father of many nations" as He had promised (Genesis 17:4-5). So we don't have to wait until some-day in the future, when everything is just right, for God to bless us with well-being. He wants to do it today!

Genesis 12:1-3

KJV—Now the Lord had said unto Abram.... I will make of thee a great nation, and I will bless thee, and make thy name great; and thou shalt be a blessing: And I will bless them that bless thee, and curse him that curseth thee: and in thee shall all families of the earth be blessed.

Amp—Now [in Haran], the Lord said to Abram....I will make of you a great nation, and I will bless you [with abundant increase of favors] and make your name famous and distinguished, and you shall be a blessing—dispensing good to others. And I will bless

those who bless you [who confer prosperity or happiness upon you], and curse him
who curses or uses insolent language toward you; in you shall all the families and
kindred of the earth be blessed—by you
they shall bless themselves.

Moffatt—Said the Eternal to Abram...."I will
make a great nation of you and bless you
and make you famous for your bliss; those
who bless you, I will bless, and anyone who
curses you I will curse, till all nations of the
world seek bliss such as yours."

NIV—The Lord had said to Abram...."I will
make you into a great nation and I will
bless you; I will make your name great, and
you will be a blessing. I will bless those who
bless you, and whoever curses you I will
curse; and all peoples on earth will be
blessed through you."

Genesis 26:1-3

KJV—And there was a famine in the land....
And the Lord appeared unto him [Isaac],
and said...Sojourn in this land, and I will be
with thee, and will bless thee; for unto thee,
and unto thy seed, I will give all these countries, and I will perform the oath which I
sware unto Abraham thy father.

Amp—And there was a famine in the land.... And the Lord appeared to him [Isaac], and said...Dwell temporarily in this land, and I will be with you and will favor you with blessings; for to you and to your descendants I will give all these lands, and I will perform the oath which I swore to Abraham your father.

Moffatt—When a famine visited the land.... The Eternal appeared to him [Isaac], saying... Reside in this land, and I will be with you and bless you [[for to you and your descendants I give all this region; I will ratify the oath I swore to your father Abraham.]]

NIV—And there was a famine in the land.... And the Lord appeared unto [Isaac], and said...Sojourn in this land, and I will be with thee, and will bless thee; for unto thee, and unto thy seed, I will give all these countries, and I will perform the oath which I sware unto Abraham thy father.

Exodus 3:7-8

KJV—The Lord said, I have surely seen the affliction of my people which are in Egypt, and have heard their cry by reason of their taskmasters; for I know their sorrows; And I am come down to deliver them out of the hand of the Egyptians, and to bring them up out of that land unto a good land and a large, unto a land flowing with milk and honey; unto the place of the Canaanites, and the Hittites, and the Amorites, and the Perizzites, and the Hivites, and the Jebusites.

Amp—The Lord said, I have surely seen the affliction of My people who are in Egypt, and have heard their cry because of their taskmasters and oppressors; for I know their sorrows and sufferings and trials. And I have come down to deliver them out of the hand and power of the Egyptians, and to bring them up out of that land to a land good and large, a land flowing with milk and honey—a land of plenty; to the place of the Canaanite, the Hittite, the Amorite, the Perizzite, the Hivite, and the Jebusite.

Moffatt—The Eternal said, "I have indeed seen the distress of my people in Egypt, I have heard them wailing under their slave-drivers; for I know their sorrows and I have come down to rescue them from the Egyptians and to bring them out of that land to a fine, large land, abounding in milk and honey, the country of the Canaanites, the Hittites, the Amorites, the Perizzites, the Hivites, and the Jebusites."

NIV—The Lord said, "I have indeed seen the misery of my people in Egypt. I have heard them crying out because of their slave drivers, and I am concerned about their suffering. So I have come down to rescue them from the hand of the Egyptians and to bring them up out of that land into a good and spacious land, a land flowing with milk and honey—the home of the Canaanites, Hittites, Amorites, Perizzites, Hivites and Jebusites."

Deuteronomy 6:18

KJV—Thou shalt do that which is right and good in the sight of the Lord: that it may be well with thee.

Amp—You shall do what is right and good in the sight of the Lord, that it may go well with you.

Moffatt—You must do whatever the Eternal holds to be right and good, that things may go well with you.

NIV—Do what is right and good in the Lord's sight, so that it may go well with you.

Nehemiah 9:21

KJV—Yea, forty years didst thou sustain them in the wilderness, so that they lacked nothing; their clothes waxed not old, and their feet swelled not.

Prosperity Is Provision, Protection and Well-being

Amp—Forty years You sustained them in the wilderness; they lacked nothing; their clothes did not wear out and their feet did not swell.

Moffatt—For forty years thou didst support them in the desert, and they lacked for nothing; their clothes never grew old, and their feet never blistered.

NIV—For forty years you sustained them in the desert; they lacked nothing, their clothes did not wear out nor did their feet become swollen.

Psalm 36:7-10

KJV—How excellent is thy lovingkindness, O God! therefore the children of men put their trust under the shadow of thy wings. They shall be abundantly satisfied with the fatness of thy house; and thou shalt make them drink of the river of thy pleasures. For with thee is the fountain of life: in thy light shall we see light. O continue thy lovingkindness unto them that know thee; and thy righteousness to the upright in heart.

Amp—How precious is Your steadfast love, O God! The children of men take refuge and put their trust under the shadow of Your wings. They relish and feast on the abundance of Your house, and You cause

them to drink of the stream of Your pleasures. For with You is the fountain of life; in
Your light do we see light. O continue Your
loving-kindness to those who know You,
Your righteousness [salvation] to the upright
in heart.

Moffatt—How precious is thy love, O God!
To thee men come for shelter in the
shadow of thy wings; they have their fill of
choice food in thy house, the stream of thy
delights to drink; for life's own fountain is
within thy presence, and in thy smile we
have the light of life. Continue thy love to
those who care for thee, thy justice to
right-minded men.

NIV—How priceless is your unfailing love!
Both high and low among men find refuge
in the shadow of your wings. They feast on
the abundance of your house; you give
them drink from your river of delights. For
with you is the fountain of life; in your light
we see light. Continue your love to those
who know you, your righteousness to the
upright in heart.

Psalm 68:19-20

KJV—Blessed be the Lord, who daily
loadeth us with benefits, even the God of
our salvation. Selah. He that is our God is

the God of salvation; and unto God the Lord belong the issues from death.

Amp—Blessed be the Lord, Who bears our burdens and carries us day by day, even the God Who is our salvation! Selah [pause, and calmly think of that]! God is to us a God of deliverances and salvation, and to God, the Lord, belongs escape from death [setting us free].

Moffatt—Blessed be the Lord, our saving God, who daily bears the burden of our life; God is for us a God of victories, thanks to the Eternal we escape from death.

NIV—Praise be to the Lord, to God our Savior, who daily bears our burdens. Selah. Our God is a God who saves; from the Sovereign Lord comes escape from death.

Psalm 103:2-5

KJV—Bless the Lord, O my soul, and forget not all his benefits: Who forgiveth all thine iniquities; who healeth all thy diseases; Who redeemeth thy life from destruction; who crowneth thee with lovingkindness and tender mercies; Who satisfieth thy mouth with good things; so that thy youth is renewed like the eagle's.

Amp—Bless—affectionately, gratefully praise—the Lord, O my soul, and all that is [deepest] within me, bless His holy name! Bless—affectionately, gratefully praise—the Lord, O my soul, and forget not [one of] all His benefits, Who forgives [every one of] all your iniquities, Who heals [each of] all your diseases; Who redeems your life from the pit and corruption; Who beautifies, dignifies and crowns you with loving-kindness and tender mercies; Who satisfies your mouth [your necessity and desire at your personal age] with good; so that your youth, renewed, is like the eagle's [strong, overcoming, soaring]!

Moffatt—Bless the Eternal, O my soul, remember all his benefits; he pardons all your sins, and all your sicknesses he heals, he saves your life from death, he crowns you with his love and pity, he gives you all your heart's desire, renewing your youth like an eagle's.

NIV—Praise the Lord, O my soul, and forget not all his benefits—who forgives all your sins and heals all your diseases, who redeems your life from the pit and crowns you with love and compassion, who satisfies your desires with good things so that your youth is renewed like the eagle's.

Psalm 107:31-32, 35-38

KJV—Oh that men would praise the Lord for his goodness, and for his wonderful works to the children of men! Let them exalt him also in the congregation of the people, and praise him in the assembly of the elders.... He turneth the wilderness into a standing water, and dry ground into watersprings. And there he maketh the hungry to dwell, that they may prepare a city for habitation; And sow the fields, and plant vineyards, which may yield fruits of increase. He blesseth them also, so that they are multiplied greatly; and suffereth not their cattle to decrease.

Amp—Oh, that men would praise [and confess to] the Lord His goodness and loving-kindness, and His wonderful works to the children of men! Let them exalt Him also in the congregation of the people, and praise Him in the company of the elders.... He turns a wilderness into a pool of water, and dry ground into water springs. And there He makes the hungry to dwell, that they may prepare a city for habitation; And sow fields, and plant vineyards, which may yield fruits of increase. He blesses them also, so that they are multiplied greatly, and allows not their cattle to decrease.

Moffatt—Let them thank the Eternal for his kindness, and for the wonders that he does for men; let them extol him, when the people meet, and praise him in the council of the sheikhs.... He turns a desert into pools of water, and dry land into fountains, where he settles famished folk, to build a town for habitation, sowing fields and planting vineyards, gathering in their harvest; by his blessing they increase, and their herds never diminish.

NIV—Let them give thanks to the Lord for his unfailing love and his wonderful deeds for men. Let them exalt him in the assembly of the people and praise him in the council of the elders.... He turned the desert into pools of water and the parched ground into flowing springs; there he brought the hungry to live, and they founded a city where they could settle. They sowed fields and planted vineyards that yielded a fruitful harvest; he blessed them, and their numbers greatly increased, and he did not let their herds diminish.

Psalm 128:1-2

KJV—Blessed is every one that feareth the Lord; that walketh in his ways. For thou shalt eat the labour of thine hands: happy shalt thou be, and it shall be well with thee.

Amp—Blessed—happy, fortunate [to be envied]—is every one who fears, reveres and worships the Lord; who walks in His ways and lives according to His commandments. For you shall eat [the fruit] of the

labor of your hands; happy, blessed, fortunate [enviable] shall you be, and it shall be
well with you.

NIV—Blessed are all who fear the Lord,
who walk in his ways. You will eat the fruit
of your labor; blessings and prosperity will
be yours.

Proverbs 10:22

KJV—The blessing of the Lord, it maketh
rich, and he addeth no sorrow with it.

Amp—The blessing of the Lord, it makes
[truly] rich, and He adds no sorrow with it,
neither does toiling increase it.

Moffatt—'Tis the Eternal's blessing that
brings wealth, and never does it bring trouble as well.

Prosperity Is
Our Inheritance

Our Lord Jesus was the greatest prosperity preacher of all. Luke 4:16-21 records His debut sermon. The message was powerful. Prosperity was the theme.

Jesus boldly declared that the Spirit of the Lord anointed Him to preach the gospel (or the good news) to the poor. What's "good news" to a poor man? You don't have to be poor anymore!

If Jesus had stopped there, we could have all shouted the victory and been blessed. But there was more. To the captives, He preached deliverance. To the brokenhearted, He brought healing. To the blind, He preached recovery of sight. The gospel Jesus proclaimed was total and complete—new birth for the spirit, restoration for the soul, healing for the body and material increase. *That's* prosperity. *That's* our inheritance. *That's* good news!

Genesis 22:16-18

KJV—By myself have I sworn, saith the Lord, for because thou hast done this thing, and hast not withheld thy son, thine only son: That in blessing I will bless thee, and in multiplying I will multiply thy seed as the stars of the heaven, and as the sand which is upon the sea shore; and thy seed shall possess the gate of his enemies; And in thy seed shall all the nations of the earth be blessed; because thou hast obeyed my voice.

Amp—I have sworn by Myself, says the Lord, since you have done this, and have not withheld [from Me] or begrudged [giving Me] your son, your only son, That in blessing I will bless you, and in multiplying I will multiply your descendants as the stars of the heavens and as the sand on the seashore. And your Seed (Heir) shall possess the gate of His enemies; And in your Seed [Christ] shall all the nations of the earth be blessed and [by Him] bless themselves, because you have heard and obeyed My voice.

Moffatt—I swear by Myself, says the Eternal, since you have done this, since you have not grudged your son, your only son, that I will indeed bless you, I will indeed make your descendants as numerous as the stars in the sky and the sand on the sea-shore; your descendants shall conquer the seats of their foes, and all nations on earth shall seek bliss like theirs—and all because you have obeyed my word.

NIV—I swear by myself, declares the Lord, that because you have done this and have not withheld your son, your only son, I will surely bless you and make your descendants as numerous as the stars in the sky and as the sand on the seashore. Your descendants will take possession of the cities of their enemies, and through your offspring all nations on earth will be blessed, because you have obeyed me.

Leviticus 20:22-24

KJV—Ye shall therefore keep all my statutes, and all my judgments, and do them: that the land, whither I bring you to dwell therein, spew you not out. And ye shall not walk in the manners of the nation, which I cast out before you: for they committed all these things, and therefore I abhorred them. But I have said unto you, Ye shall inherit their land, and I will give it unto you to possess it, a land that floweth with milk and honey: I am the Lord your God, which have separated you from other people.

Amp—You shall therefore keep all My statutes and all My ordinances, and do them; that the land where I am bringing you to dwell may not vomit you out [as it did those before you]. You shall not walk in the customs of the nation which I am casting out before you; for they did all these things, and therefore I was wearied and grieved by them. But I have said to you, You shall inherit their land, and I will give it to you to possess, a land flowing with milk and honey. I am the Lord your God, Who has separated you from the peoples.

Moffatt—Well, then, keep all my rules and regulations obediently, lest the land where I have brought you to live vomit you out. You must not live by the customs of the nations I expelled before you; I abhorred them just because they practised all these crimes. But to you I have said, "You shall inherit their land, I assign it to you as your own, a land abounding in milk and honey: I am the Eternal your God, who have separated you from other races."

NIV—Keep all my decrees and laws and follow them, so that the land where I am bringing you to live may not vomit you out. You must not live according to the customs of the nations I am going to drive out before you. Because they did all these things, I abhorred them. But I said to you, "You will possess their land; I will give it to you as an inheritance, a land flowing with milk and honey." I am the Lord your God, who has set you apart from the nations.

Deuteronomy 28:1-11

KJV—It shall come to pass, if thou shalt hearken diligently unto the voice of the Lord thy God, to observe and to do all his commandments which I command thee this day, that the Lord thy God will set thee on high above all nations of the earth: And all these blessings shall come on thee, and overtake thee, if thou shalt hearken unto the voice of the Lord thy God.

Blessed shalt thou be in the city, and blessed shalt thou be in the field. Blessed shall be the fruit of thy body, and the fruit of thy ground, and the fruit of thy cattle, the increase of thy kine, and the flocks of thy sheep. Blessed shall be thy basket and thy store. Blessed shalt thou be when thou comest in, and blessed shalt thou be when thou goest out.

The Lord shall cause thine enemies that rise up against thee to be smitten before thy face: they shall come out against thee one way, and flee before thee seven ways. The Lord shall command the blessing upon thee in thy storehouses, and in all that thou settest thine hand unto; and he shall bless thee in the land which the Lord thy God giveth thee.

The Lord shall establish thee an holy people unto himself, as he hath sworn unto thee, if thou shalt keep the commandments of the Lord thy God, and walk in his ways. And all people of the earth shall see that thou art called by the name of the Lord; and they shall be afraid of thee.

And the Lord shall make thee plenteous in goods, in the fruit of thy body, and in the fruit of thy cattle, and in the fruit of thy ground, in the land which the Lord sware unto thy fathers to give thee.

Amp—If you will listen diligently to the voice of the Lord your God, being watchful to do all His commandments which I command you this day, the Lord your God will set you high above all the nations of the earth, And all these blessings shall come upon you and overtake you, if you heed the voice of the Lord your God.

Blessed shall you be in the city, and blessed shall you be in the field. Blessed shall be the fruit of your body, and the fruit of your ground, and the fruit of your beasts, the increase of your cattle, and the young of your flock. Blessed shall be your basket and your kneading trough. Blessed shall you be when you come in, and blessed shall you be when you go out.

The Lord shall cause your enemies who rise up against you to be defeated before your face; they shall come out against you one way, and flee before you seven ways. The Lord shall command the blessing upon you in your storehouse, and in all that you undertake; and He will bless you in the land which the Lord your God gives you.

The Lord will establish you as a people holy to Himself, as He has sworn to you, if you keep the commandments of the Lord your God, and walk in His ways. And all people of the earth shall see that you are called by the name [and in the presence of] the Lord; and they shall be afraid of you.

And the Lord shall make you have a surplus of prosperity, through the fruit of your body, of your livestock, and of your ground, in the land which the Lord swore to your fathers to give you.

Moffatt—If only you will listen carefully to what the Eternal your God orders, mindful to carry out all his commands which I enjoin upon you this day, then the Eternal your God will lift you high above all the nations of the earth, and all these blessings shall come upon you and overtake you, if only you listen to the voice of the Eternal your God.

You shall be blessed in town and in country; blessed shall be the fruit of your body and of your ground, the young of your cattle and the lambs of your flock; full shall your basket be, and your kneading-trough; blessed shall you be as you start out and as you come home.

The foes who attack you the Eternal will rout before you; they may assail you all together, but they shall fly before you in all directions. The Eternal will command you to be blessed in your barns and in every enterprise to which you put your hand, blessing you in the land which the Eternal your God assigns to you.

The Eternal will confirm your position as a people sacred to himself, as he swore to you, if you obey the orders of the Eternal your God and live his life, so that when all nations on earth see you are owned by the Eternal, they may stand in awe of you.

The Eternal will make you overflow with prosperity in the fruit of your body, of your cattle, and of your ground, the ground that the Eternal swore to your fathers that he would give you.

NIV—If you fully obey the Lord your God and carefully follow all his commands I give you today, the Lord your God will set you high above all the nations on earth. All these blessings will come upon you and accompany you if you obey the Lord your God:

You will be blessed in the city and blessed in the country. The fruit of your womb will be blessed, and the crops of your land and the young of your livestock—the calves of your herds and the lambs of your flocks. Your basket and your kneading trough will be blessed. You will be blessed when you come in and blessed when you go out.

The Lord will grant that the enemies who rise up against you will be defeated before you. They will come at you from one direction but flee from you in seven. The Lord will send a blessing on your barns and on everything you put your hand to. The Lord your God will bless you in the land he is giving you.

The Lord will establish you as his holy people, as he promised you on oath, if you keep the commands of the Lord your God and walk in his ways. Then all the peoples on earth will see that you are called by the name of the Lord, and they will fear you.

The Lord will grant you abundant prosperity—in the fruit of your womb, the young of your livestock and the crops of your ground—in the land he swore to your forefathers to give you.

Deuteronomy 28:13

KJV—The Lord shall make thee the head, and not the tail; and thou shalt be above only, and thou shalt not be beneath; if that thou hearken unto the commandments of the Lord thy God, which I command thee this day, to observe and to do them.

Prosperity Is Our Inheritance

Amp—The Lord shall make you the head, and not the tail; and you shall be above only, and you shall not be beneath, if you heed the commandments of the Lord your God, which I command you this day, and are watchful to do them.

Moffatt—So shall the Eternal put you at the head, not at the tail; you shall be always rising, never falling, as you listen to the commands of the Eternal your God which I enjoin upon you this day, and carry them out carefully.

NIV—The Lord will make you the head, not the tail. If you pay attention to the commands of the Lord your God that I give you this day and carefully follow them, you will always be at the top, never at the bottom.

Psalm 37:11

KJV—The meek shall inherit the earth; and shall delight themselves in the abundance of peace.

Amp—The meek [in the end] shall inherit the earth, and shall delight themselves in the abundance of peace.

Moffatt—The land will be left to the humble, to enjoy plenteous prosperity.

NIV—The meek will inherit the land and enjoy great peace.

Proverbs 13:22

KJV—A good man leaveth an inheritance to his children's children: and the wealth of the sinner is laid up for the just.

Amp—A good man leaves an inheritance [of moral stability and goodness] to his children's children, and the wealth of the sinner [finds its way eventually] into the hands of the righteous, for whom it was laid up.

Moffatt—A pious man leaves wealth to his children's children: the sinner lays up treasure—to enrich the good!

NIV—A good man leaves an inheritance for his children's children, but a sinner's wealth is stored up for the righteous.

Matthew 19:29

KJV—Every one that hath forsaken houses, or brethren, or sisters, or father, or mother, or wife, or children, or lands, for my name's sake, shall receive an hundredfold, and shall inherit everlasting life.

Amp—Any one and every one who has left houses or brothers or sisters or father or

179

*Prosperity
Is Our
Inheritance*

mother or children or lands for My name's sake, will receive many—even a hundred—times more, and inherit eternal life.

Moffatt—Everyone who has left brothers or sisters or father or mother or wife or children or lands or houses for my name's sake will get a hundred times as much and inherit life eternal.

NIV—Everyone who has left houses or brothers or sisters or father or mother or children or fields for my sake will receive a hundred times as much and will inherit eternal life.

Luke 4:18

KJV—The Spirit of the Lord is upon me, because he hath anointed me to preach the gospel to the poor; he hath sent me to heal the brokenhearted, to preach deliverance to the captives, and recovering of sight to the blind, to set at liberty them that are bruised.

Amp—The Spirit of the Lord [is] upon Me, because He has anointed Me [the Anointed One, the Messiah] to preach the good news (the Gospel) to the poor; He has sent Me to announce release to the captives, and recovery of sight to the blind; to send forth delivered those who are oppressed—who are downtrodden, bruised, crushed and broken down by calamity.

Moffatt—The Spirit of the Lord is upon me: for he has consecrated me to preach the gospel to the poor, he has sent me to proclaim release for captives and recovery of sight for the blind, to set free the oppressed.

NIV—The Spirit of the Lord is on me, because he has anointed me to preach good news to the poor. He has sent me to proclaim freedom for the prisoners and recovery of sight for the blind, to release the oppressed.

2 Corinthians 8:9

KJV—For ye know the grace of our Lord Jesus Christ, that, though he was rich, yet for your sakes he became poor, that ye through his poverty might be rich.

Amp—For you are coming progressively to be acquainted with and to recognize more strongly and clearly the grace of our Lord Jesus Christ—His kindness, His gracious generosity, His undeserved favor and spiritual blessing; [in] that though He was [so very] rich, yet for your sakes He became [so very] poor, in order that by His poverty you might become enriched—abundantly supplied.

Moffatt—You know how gracious our Lord Jesus Christ was; rich though he was, he became poor for the sake of you, that by his poverty you might be rich.

NIV—For you know the grace of our Lord Jesus Christ, that though he was rich, yet for your sakes he became poor, so that you through his poverty might become rich.

Galatians 3:13-14, 29

KJV—Christ hath redeemed us from the curse of the law, being made a curse for us: for it is written, Cursed is every one that hangeth on a tree: That the blessing of Abraham might come on the Gentiles through Jesus Christ; that we might receive the promise of the Spirit through faith....

And if ye be Christ's, then are ye Abraham's seed, and heirs according to the promise.

Amp—Christ purchased our freedom (redeeming us) from the curse (doom) of the Law's (condemnation), by [Himself] becoming a curse for us, for it is written [in the Scriptures], Cursed is everyone who hangs on a tree (is crucified); To the end that through [their receiving] Christ Jesus, the blessing [promised] to Abraham might come upon the Gentiles, so that we through faith might [all] receive [the realization of] the promise of the (Holy) Spirit....

And if you belong to Christ (are in Him, Who is Abraham's Seed), then you are Abraham's offspring and (spiritual) heirs according to promise.

Moffatt—Christ ransomed us from the curse of the Law by becoming accursed for us (for it is written, Cursed is everyone who hangs on a gibbet), that the blessing of Abraham might reach the Gentiles in Christ Jesus, so that by faith we might receive the promised Spirit....

Now if you are Christ's, then you are Abraham's offspring; in virtue of the Promise, you are heirs.

NIV—Christ redeemed us from the curse of the law by becoming a curse for us, for it is written: "Cursed is everyone who is hung on a tree." He redeemed us in order that the blessing given to Abraham might come to the Gentiles through Christ Jesus, so that by faith we might receive the promise of the Spirit....

If you belong to Christ, then you are Abraham's seed, and heirs according to the promise.

Ephesians 1:17-23
(Pray this for yourself!)

KJV—That the God of our Lord Jesus Christ, the Father of glory, may give unto you the spirit of wisdom and revelation in the knowledge of him: The eyes of your understanding being enlightened; that ye may know what is the hope of his calling, and what the riches of the glory of his inheritance in the saints, And what is the exceeding greatness of his power to us-ward who believe, according to the working of his mighty power, Which he wrought in Christ, when he raised him from the dead, and set him at his own right hand in the heavenly places, Far above all principality, and power, and might, and dominion, and every name that is named, not only in this world, but also in that which is to come: And hath put all things under his feet, and gave him to be the head over all things to the church, Which is his body, the fulness of him that filleth all in all.

Amp—[For I always pray] the God of our Lord Jesus Christ, the Father of Glory, that He may grant you a spirit of wisdom and revelation—of insight into mysteries and secrets—in the [deep and intimate] knowledge of him, By having the eyes of your heart flooded with light, so that you can know and understand the hope to which He has called you and how rich is His glorious inheritance in the saints—His set-apart ones. And [so that you can know and understand] what is the immeasurable and unlimited and surpassing greatness of His power in and for us who believe, as demonstrated in the working of His mighty strength, Which He exerted in Christ when He raised Him from the dead and seated Him at His [own] right hand in the heavenly [places], Far above all rule and authority and power and dominion, and every name that is named—above every title that can be conferred—not only in this age and in this world, but also in the age and the world which are to come. And He has put all things under His feet and has appointed Him the universal and supreme Head of the church (a headship exercised throughout the church), Which is His body, the fullness of Him Who fills all in all—for in that body lives the full measure of Him Who makes everything complete, and Who fills everything everywhere [with Himself].

Moffatt—May the God of our Lord Jesus Christ, the glorious Father, grant you the Spirit of wisdom and the revelation for the knowledge of himself, illuminating the eyes of your heart so that you can understand the hope to which He calls us, the wealth of his glorious heritage in the saints, and the surpassing greatness of his power over us believers—a power which operates with the strength of the might which he exerted in raising Christ from the dead and seating him at his right hand in the heavenly sphere, above all the angelic Rulers, Authorities, Powers, and Lords, above every Name that is to be named not only in this age but in the age to come—he has put everything under his feet and set him as head over everything for the church, the church which is his Body, filled by him who fills the universe entirely.

NIV—I keep asking that the God of our Lord Jesus Christ, the glorious Father, may give you the Spirit of wisdom and revelation, so that you may know him better. I pray also that the eyes of your heart may be enlightened in order that you may know the hope to which he has called you, the riches of his glorious inheritance in the saints, and his incomparably great power for us who believe. That power is like the working of his mighty strength, which he exerted in Christ when he raised him from the dead and seated him at his right hand in the heavenly realms, far above all rule and authority, power and dominion, and every title that can be given, not only in the present age but also in the one to come. And God placed all things under his feet and appointed him to be head over everything for the church, which is his body, the fullness of him who fills everything in every way.

Colossians 3:23-24

KJV—Whatsoever ye do, do it heartily, as to the Lord, and not unto men; Knowing that of the Lord ye shall receive the reward of the inheritance: for ye serve the Lord Christ.

Amp—Whatever may be your task, work at it heartily (from the soul), as [something done] for the Lord and not for men, Knowing (with all certainty) that it is from the Lord [and not from men] that you will receive the inheritance which is your (real) reward. [The One Whom] you are actually serving [is] the Lord Christ, the Messiah.

*Prosperity
Is Our
Inheritance*

Moffatt—Whatever be your task, work at it heartily, as servants of the Lord and not of men; remember, you are to receive from the Lord the inheritance which is your due; serve Christ your Lord and Master.

NIV—Whatever you do, work at it with all your heart, as working for the Lord, not for men, since you know that you will receive an inheritance from the Lord as a reward. It is the Lord Christ you are serving.

1 Timothy 6:17-19

KJV—Charge them that are rich in this world, that they be not highminded, nor trust in uncertain riches, but in the living

God, who giveth us richly all things to enjoy; that they do good, that they be rich in good works, ready to distribute, willing to communicate; laying up in store for themselves a good foundation against the time to come, that they may lay hold on eternal life.

Amp—As for the rich in this world, charge them not to be proud and arrogant and contemptuous of others, nor to set their hopes on uncertain riches but on God, Who richly and ceaselessly provides us with everything for [our] enjoyment; [Charge them] to do good, to be rich in good works, to be liberal and generous-hearted, ready to share [with others], In this way laying up for themselves [the riches that endure forever] a good foundation for the future, so that they may grasp that which is life indeed.

Moffatt—Charge the rich of this world not to be supercilious, and not to fix their hopes on so uncertain a thing as riches but on the living God who richly provides us with all the joys of life; bid them be bountiful, rich in good works, open-handed and generous, amassing right good treasure for themselves in the world to come, so as to secure the life which is life indeed.

NIV—Command those who are rich in this present world not to be arrogant nor to put their hope in wealth, which is so uncertain, but to put their hope in God, who richly provides us with everything for our enjoyment. Command them to do good, to be rich in good deeds, and to be generous and willing to share. In this way they will lay up treasure for themselves as a firm foundation for the coming age, so that they may take hold of the life that is truly life.

1 Peter 3:9-12

KJV—Not rendering evil for evil, or railing for railing: but contrariwise blessing; knowing that ye are thereunto called, that ye should inherit a blessing. For he that will love life, and see good days, let him refrain his tongue from evil, and his lips that they speak no guile: Let him eschew evil, and do good; let him seek peace, and ensue it. For the eyes of the Lord are over the righteous, and his ears are open unto their prayers: but the face of the Lord is against them that do evil.

Amp—Never return evil for evil or insult for insult—scolding, tongue-lashing, berating; but on the contrary blessing—praying for their welfare, happiness and protection, and truly pitying and loving them. For know that to this you have been called, that you may yourselves inherit a blessing [from God]— obtain a blessing as heirs, bringing welfare and happiness and protection.

For let him who wants to enjoy life and see good days (good whether apparent or not), keep his tongue free from evil, and his lips from guile (treachery, deceit). Let him turn away from wickedness and shun it; and let him do right. Let him search for peace—harmony, undisturbedness from fears, agitating passions and moral conflicts—and seek it eagerly.—Do not merely desire peaceful relations [with God, with your fellowmen, and with yourself], but pursue, go after them! For the eyes of the Lord are upon the righteous—those who are upright and in right standing with God—and His ears are attentive to their prayer. But the face of the Lord is against those who practice evil—to oppose them, to frustrate and defeat them.

Moffatt—Never paying back evil for evil, never reviling when you are reviled, but on the contrary blessing. For this is your vocation, to bless and to inherit blessing; he who would love Life and enjoy good days, let him keep his tongue from evil and his lips from speaking guile: let him shun wrong and do right, let him seek peace, making peace his aim. For the eyes of the Lord are on the upright, and his ears are open to their cry; but the face of the Lord is set against wrongdoers.

NIV—Do not repay evil with evil or insult with insult, but with blessing, because to this you were called so that you may inherit a blessing. For, "Whoever would love life and see good days must keep his tongue from evil and his lips from deceitful speech. He must turn from evil and do good; he must seek peace and pursue it. For the eyes of the Lord are on the righteous and his ears are attentive to their prayer, but the face of the Lord is against those who do evil."

2 Peter 1:3-11

KJV—According as his divine power hath given unto us all things that pertain unto life and godliness, through the knowledge of him that hath called us to glory and virtue: Whereby are given unto us exceeding great and precious promises: that by these ye might be partakers of the divine nature, having escaped the corruption that is in the world through lust. And beside this, giving all diligence, add to your faith virtue; and to virtue knowledge; and to knowledge temperance; and to temperance patience; and to patience godliness; and to godliness brotherly kindness; and to brotherly kindness charity.

For if these things be in you, and abound, they make you that ye shall neither be barren nor unfruitful in the knowledge of our Lord Jesus Christ. But he that lacketh these things is blind, and cannot see afar off, and hath forgotten that he was purged from his old sins.

Wherefore the rather, brethren, give diligence to make your calling and election sure: for if ye do these things, ye shall never fall: For so an entrance shall be ministered unto you abundantly into the everlasting kingdom of our Lord and Saviour Jesus Christ.

Amp—For his divine power has bestowed upon us all things that [are requisite and suited] to life and godliness, through the (full, personal) knowledge of Him Who called us by and to His own glory and excellence (virtue). By means of these He has bestowed on us His precious and exceedingly great promises, so that through them you may escape (by flight) from the moral decay (rottenness and corruption) that is in the world because of covetousness (lust and greed), and become sharers (partakers) of the divine nature. For this very reason, adding your diligence [to the divine promises], employ every effort in exercising your faith to develop virtue (excellence, resolution, Christian energy); and in [exercising] virtue [develop] knowledge (intelligence), And in [exercising] knowledge [develop] self-control; and in [exercising] self-control [develop] steadfastness (patience, endurance), and in [exercising] steadfastness [develop] godliness (piety), And in [exercising] godliness [develop] brotherly affection, and in |exercising| brotherly affection |develop| Christian love.

For as these qualities are yours and increasingly abound in you, they will keep |you| from being idle or unfruitful unto the (full personal) knowledge of our Lord Jesus Christ, the Messiah, the Anointed One. For whoever lacks these qualities is blind, |spiritually| short-sighted, seeing only what is near to him; and has become oblivious |of the fact| that he was cleansed from his old sins.

Because of this, brethren, be all the more solicitous and eager to make sure (to ratify, to strengthen, to make steadfast) your calling and election; for if you do this you will never stumble or fall. Thus there will be richly and abundantly provided for you entry into the eternal kingdom of our Lord and Savior Jesus Christ.

Moffatt—Inasmuch as his power divine has bestowed upon us every requisite for life and godliness by the knowledge of him who called us to his own•glory and excellence— bestowing on us thereby promises precious and supreme, that by means of them you may escape the corruption produced within the world by lust, and participate in the divine nature—for this very reason, do you contrive to make it your whole concern to furnish your faith with resolution, resolution with intelligence, intelligence with self-control, self-control with stedfastness, stedfastness with godliness, godliness with brotherliness, and brotherliness with Christian love.

For as these qualities exist and increase with you, they render you active and fruitful in the knowledge of our Lord Jesus Christ; whereas he who has not these by him is blind, short-sighted, oblivious that he has been cleansed from his erstwhile sins.

So be the more eager, brothers, to ratify your calling and election, for as you exercise these qualities you will never make a slip; you will thus be richly furnished with the right of entry into the eternal realm of our Lord and saviour Jesus Christ.

NIV—His divine power has given us everything we need for life and godliness through our knowledge of him who called us by his own glory and goodness. Through these he has given us his very great and precious promises, so that through them you may participate in the divine nature and escape the corruption in the world caused by evil desires. For this very reason, make every effort to add to your faith goodness; and to goodness, knowledge; and to knowledge, self-control; and to self-control, perseverance; and to perseverance, godliness; and to godliness, brotherly kindness; and to brotherly kindness, love.

For if you possess these qualities in increasing measure, they will keep you from being ineffective and unproductive in your knowledge of our Lord Jesus Christ. But if anyone does not have them, he is nearsighted and blind, and has forgotten that he has been cleansed from his past sins.

Therefore, my brothers, be all the more eager to make your calling and election sure. For if you do these things, you will never fall, and you will receive a rich welcome into the eternal kingdom of our Lord and Savior Jesus Christ.

Prosperity Is Our Inheritance

What Jesus Said
About Prosperity

We can't pretend that money isn't important. It *is* important. Jesus said where our treasure is (which includes our money), there will our heart be also (Matthew 6:21). He fully understood that people will invest in what is close to their heart. So where and how we spend our money tells a lot about our priorities and what's most important to us.

The attitude of our heart and our motives determine whether our giving pleases God or not. In Malachi, it says He rejected Israel's offering because they brought Him defective animals—blind calves and injured ones they couldn't use. God said it offended Him. But in 2 Corinthians 9:7, *The Amplified Bible* says, "God loves (*that is, He takes pleasure in, prizes above other things, and is unwilling to abandon or to do without*) *a cheerful* (*joyous, prompt-to-do-it*) *giver—whose heart is in his giving.*"

The entire kingdom of God is governed by the law of sowing and reaping. But it's not enough just to give. What matters most is *how* and *why* we give. That's why Jesus emphasized the attitude of heart when He taught on the importance of giving.

Matthew 6:3-6

KJV—When thou doest alms, let not thy left hand know what thy right hand doeth: that thine alms may be in secret: and thy Father which seeth in secret himself shall reward thee openly. And when thou prayest, thou shalt not be as the hypocrites are: for they love to pray standing in the synagogues and in the corners of the streets, that they may be seen of men. Verily I say unto you, They have their reward. But thou, when thou prayest, enter into thy closet, and when thou hast shut thy door, pray to thy Father which is in secret; and thy Father which seeth in secret shall reward thee openly.

Amp—When you give to charity, do not let your left hand know what your right hand is doing, So that your deeds of charity may be in secret; and your Father Who sees in secret will reward you openly. Also when you pray you must not be like the hypocrites, for they love to pray standing in the synagogues and on the corners of the streets, that they may be seen by people. Truly, I tell you, they have their reward—in full already. But when you pray, go into your most private room, and closing the door, pray to your Father Who is in secret; and your Father Who sees in secret will reward you in the open.

Moffatt—When you give alms, never let your left hand know what your right hand is doing, so as to keep your alms secret; then your Father who sees what is secret will reward you openly. Also, when you pray, you must not be like the hypocrites, for they like to stand and pray in the synagogues and at the street-corners, so as to be seen by men; I tell you truly, they do get their reward. When you pray, go into your room and shut the door, pray to your Father who is in secret, and your Father who sees what is secret will reward you.

NIV—When you give to the needy, do not let your left hand know what your right hand is doing, so that your giving may be in secret. Then your Father, who sees what is done in secret, will reward you. And when you pray, do not be like the hypocrites, for they love to pray standing in the synagogues and on the street corners to be seen by men. I tell you the truth, they have received their reward in full. But when you pray, go into your room, close the door and pray to your

Father, who is unseen. Then your Father, who sees what is done in secret, will reward you.

Matthew 6:19-21

KJV—Lay not up for yourselves treasures upon earth, where moth and rust doth corrupt, and where thieves break through and steal: But lay up for yourselves treasures in heaven, where neither moth nor rust doth corrupt, and where thieves do not break through nor steal: For where your treasure is, there will your heart be also.

Amp—Do not gather and heap up and store for yourselves treasures on earth, where moth and rust and worm consume and destroy, and where thieves break through and steal; But gather and heap up and store for yourselves treasures in heaven, where neither moth nor rust nor worm consume and destroy, and where thieves do not break through and steal; For where your treasure is, there will your heart be also.

Moffatt—Store up no treasures for yourselves on earth, where moth and rust corrode, where thieves break in and steal: store up treasures for yourselves in heaven, where neither moth nor rust corrode, where thieves do not break in and steal. For where your treasure lies, your heart will lie there too.

NIV—Do not store up for yourselves treasures on earth, where moth and rust destroy, and where thieves break in and steal. But store up for yourselves treasures in heaven, where moth and rust do not destroy, and where thieves do not break in and steal. For where your treasure is, there your heart will be also.

Matthew 6:25-26, 28, 30, 32-33

KJV—Therefore I say unto you, Take no thought for your life, what ye shall eat, or what ye shall drink; nor yet for your body, what ye shall put on. Is not the life more than meat, and the body than raiment? Behold the fowls of the air: for they sow not, neither do they reap, nor gather into barns; yet your heavenly Father feedeth them. Are ye not much better than they?...

And why take ye thought for raiment? Consider the lilies of the field, how they grow; they toil not, neither do they spin.... Wherefore, if God so clothe the grass of the field, which today is, and tomorrow is cast into the oven, shall he not much more clothe you, O ye of little faith?...

(For after all these things do the Gentiles seek:) for your heavenly Father knoweth that ye have need of all these things. But seek ye first the kingdom of God, and his righteousness; and all these things shall be added unto you.

Amp—Therefore I tell you, stop being perpetually uneasy (anxious and worried) about your life, what you shall eat or what you shall drink, and about your body, what you shall put on. Is not life greater [in quality] than food, and the body [far above and more excellent] than clothing? Look at the birds of the air; they neither sow nor reap nor gather into barns, and yet your heavenly Father keeps feeding them. Are you not worth more than they?...

And why should you be anxious about clothes? Consider the lilies of the field and learn thoroughly how they grow; they neither toil nor spin.... But if God so clothes the grass of the field, which today is alive and green and tomorrow is tossed into the furnace, will He not much more surely clothe you, O you men with little faith?...

For the Gentiles (heathen) wish for and crave and diligently seek after all these things; and your heavenly Father well knows that you need them all. But seek for (aim at and strive after) first of all His kingdom, and His righteousness [His way of doing and being right], and then all these things taken together will be given you besides.

Moffatt—Therefore I tell you, never trouble about what you are to eat or drink in life, nor about what you are to put on your body; surely life means more than food, surely the body means more than clothes!

Look at the wild birds; they sow not, they reap not, they gather nothing in granaries, and yet your heavenly Father feeds them. Are you not worth more than birds?...

And why should you trouble over clothing? Look how the lilies of the field grow; they neither toil nor spin.... Now if God so clothes the grass of the field which blooms to-day and is thrown to-morrow into the furnace, will not he much more clothe you? O men, how little you trust him!...

(Pagans make all that their aim in life) for well your heavenly Father knows you need all that. Seek God's Realm and his goodness, and all that will be yours over and above.

NIV—Therefore I tell you, do not worry about your life, what you will eat or drink; or about your body, what you will wear. Is not life more important than food, and the body more important than clothes? Look at the birds of the air; they do not sow or reap or store away in barns, and yet your heavenly Father feeds them. Are you not much more valuable than they?...

And why do you worry about clothes? See how the lilies of the field grow. They do not labor or spin.... If that is how God clothes the grass of the field, which is here today and tomorrow is thrown into the fire, will he not much more clothe you, O you of little faith?...

For the pagans run after all these things, and your heavenly Father knows that you need them. But seek first his kingdom and his righteousness, and all these things will be given to you as well.

Matthew 7:7-11

KJV—Ask, and it shall be given you; seek, and ye shall find; knock, and it shall be opened unto you: For every one that asketh receiveth; and he that seeketh findeth; and to him that knocketh it shall be opened. Or what man is there of you, whom if his son ask bread, will he give him a stone? Or if he ask a fish, will he give him a serpent? If ye then, being evil, know how to give good gifts unto your children, how much more shall your Father which is in heaven give good things to them that ask him?

Amp—Keep on asking and it will be given you; keep on seeking and you will find; keep on knocking [reverently] and the door will be opened to you. For every one who keeps on asking receives, and he who keeps on seeking finds, and to him who keeps on knocking it will be opened. Or what man is there of you, if his son asks him for a loaf of bread, will hand him a stone? Or if he asks for a fish, will hand him a serpent? If you then, evil as you are, know how to give good and advantageous gifts to your children, how much more will your Father Who is in heaven [perfect as He is] give good and advantageous things to those who keep on asking Him!

Moffatt—Ask and the gift will be yours, seek and you will find, knock and the door will open to you; for everyone who asks receives, the seeker finds, the door is opened to anyone who knocks. Why, which of you, when asked by his son for a loaf, will hand him a stone? Or, if he asks a fish, will you hand him a serpent? Well, if for all your evil you know to give your children what is good, how much more will your Father in heaven give good to those who ask him?

NIV—Ask and it will be given to you; seek and you will find; knock and the door will be opened to you. For everyone who asks receives; he who seeks finds; and to him who knocks, the door will be opened. Which of you, if his son asks for bread, will give him a stone? Or if he asks for a fish, will give him a snake? If you, then, though you are evil, know how to give good gifts to your children, how much more will your Father in heaven give good gifts to those who ask him!

Matthew 10:8

KJV—Heal the sick, cleanse the lepers, raise the dead, cast out devils: freely ye have received, freely give.

Amp—Cure the sick; raise the dead; cleanse the lepers; drive out demons. Freely (without pay) you have received; freely (without charge) give.

Moffatt—Heal the sick, raise the dead, cleanse lepers, cast out demons; give without being paid, as you have got without paying.

NIV—Heal the sick, raise the dead, cleanse those who have leprosy, drive out demons. Freely you have received, freely give.

Matthew 10:41-42

KJV—He that receiveth a prophet in the name of a prophet shall receive a prophet's reward; and he that receiveth a righteous man in the name of a righteous man shall receive a righteous man's reward. And whosoever shall give to drink unto one of these little ones a cup of cold water only in the name of a disciple, verily I say unto you, he shall in no wise lose his reward.

Amp—He who receives and welcomes and accepts a prophet because he is a prophet shall receive a prophet's reward, and he who receives and welcomes and accepts a righteous man because he is a righteous man shall receive a righteous man's reward. And whoever gives to one of these little ones [in rank or influence] even a cup of cold water because he is My disciple, surely, I declare to you, he shall not lose his reward.

Moffatt—He who receives a prophet because he is a prophet, will receive a prophet's reward; he who receives a good man because he is good, will receive a good man's reward. And whoever gives one of these little ones even a cup of cold water because he is a disciple, I tell you, he shall not lose his reward.

NIV—Anyone who receives a prophet because he is a prophet will receive a prophet's reward, and anyone who receives a righteous man because he is a righteous man will receive a righteous man's reward. And if anyone gives even a cup of cold water to one of these little ones because he is my disciple, I tell you the truth, he will certainly not lose his reward.

Matthew 21:21-22

KJV—Jesus answered and said unto them, Verily I say unto you, If ye have faith, and doubt not, ye shall not only do this which is done to the fig tree, but also if ye shall say unto this mountain, Be thou removed, and be thou cast into the sea; it shall be done. And all things, whatsoever ye shall ask in prayer, believing, ye shall receive.

Amp—Jesus answered them, Truly, I say to you, if you have faith—a firm relying trust—and do not doubt, you will not only do what has been done to the fig tree, but even if you say to this mountain, Be taken up and cast into the sea, it will be done. And whatever you ask for in prayer, having faith and [really] believing, you will receive.

Moffatt—Jesus answered, "I tell you truly, if you have faith, if you have no doubt, you will not only do what has been done to the fig tree, but even if you say to this hill, 'Take and throw yourself into the sea,' it will be done. All that ever you ask in prayer you shall have, if you believe."

NIV—Jesus replied, "I tell you the truth, if you have faith and do not doubt, not only can you do what was done to the fig tree, but also you can say to this mountain, 'Go, throw yourself into the sea,' and it will be done. If you believe, you will receive whatever you ask for in prayer."

Matthew 25:31-40

KJV—When the Son of man shall come in his glory, and all the holy angels with him, then shall he sit upon the throne of his glory: And before him shall be gathered all nations: and he shall separate them one from another, as a shepherd divideth his sheep from the goats: And he shall set the sheep on his right hand, but the goats on the left.

Then shall the King say unto them on his right hand, Come, ye blessed of my Father, inherit the kingdom prepared for you from the foundation of the world: For I was an hungered, and ye gave me meat: I was thirsty, and ye gave me drink: I was a stranger, and ye took me in: Naked, and ye clothed me: I was sick, and ye visited me: I was in prison, and ye came unto me.

Then shall the righteous answer him, saying, Lord, when saw we thee an hungered, and fed thee? or thirsty, and gave thee drink? When saw we thee a stranger, and took thee in? or naked, and clothed thee? Or when saw we thee sick, or in prison, and came unto thee?

And the King shall answer and say unto them, Verily I say unto you, Inasmuch as ye have done it unto one of the least of these my brethren, ye have done it unto me.

Amp—When the Son of man comes in His glory (His majesty and splendor) and all the holy angels with Him, then He will sit on the throne of His glory. All nations shall be gathered before Him, and He will separate them [the people] from one another as a shepherd separates his sheep from the goats, And He will cause the sheep to stand at His right hand, but the goats at His left.

What Jesus Said About Prosperity

Then the King will say to those at His right hand, Come, you blessed of My Father [that is, you favored of God and appointed to eternal salvation], inherit—receive as your own—the kingdom prepared for you from the foundation of the world. For I was hungry and you gave Me food; I was thirsty and you gave Me something to drink; I was a stranger and you brought Me together with yourselves and welcomed and entertained and lodged Me; I was naked and you clothed Me; I was sick and you visited Me with help and ministering care; I was in prison and you came to see Me.

Then the just and upright will answer Him, Lord, when did we see You hungry and gave You food, or thirsty and gave You something to drink? And when did we see You a stranger and welcomed and entertained You, or naked and clothed You? And when did we see You sick or in prison and came to visit You?

And the King will reply to them, Truly, I tell you, in as far as you did it to one of the least [in the estimation of men] of these My brethren, you did it to Me.

Moffatt—When the Son of man comes in his glory, and all the angels with him, then he will sit on the throne of his glory, and all nations will be gathered in front of him; he will separate them one from another, as a shepherd separates the sheep from the goats, setting the sheep on his right hand and the goats on his left.

Then shall the King say to those on his right, "Come, you whom my Father has blessed, come into your inheritance in the realm prepared for you from the foundation of the world. For I was hungry and you fed me, I was thirsty and you gave me drink, I was a stranger and you entertained me, I was unclothed and you clothed me, I was ill and you looked after me, I was in prison and you visited me."

Then the just will answer, "Lord, when did we see you hungry and feed you? or thirsty and gave you drink? when did we see you a stranger and entertain you? or unclothed and clothed you? when did we see you ill or in prison and visit you?"

The King will answer them, "I tell you truly, in so far as you did it to one of these my brothers, even to the least of them, you did it to me."

NIV—When the Son of Man comes in his glory, and all the angels with him, he will sit on his throne in heavenly glory. All the nations will be gathered before him, and he will separate the people one from another as a shepherd separates the sheep from the goats. He will put the sheep on his right and the goats on his left.

Then the King will say to those on his right, "Come, you who are blessed by my

Father; take your inheritance, the kingdom prepared for you since the creation of the world. For I was hungry and you gave me something to eat, I was thirsty and you gave me something to drink, I was a stranger and you invited me in, I needed clothes and you clothed me, I was sick and you looked after me, I was in prison and you came to visit me."

Then the righteous will answer him, "Lord, when did we see you hungry and feed you, or thirsty and give you something to drink? When did we see you a stranger and invite you in, or needing clothes and clothe you? When did we see you sick or in prison and go to visit you?"

The King will reply, "I tell you the truth, whatever you did for one of the least of these brothers of mine, you did for me."

Mark 4:20-25

KJV—These are they which are sown on good ground; such as hear the word, and receive it, and bring forth fruit, some thirty-fold, some sixty, and some an hundred. And he said unto them, Is a candle brought to be put under a bushel, or under a bed? and not to be set on a candlestick? For there is nothing hid, which shall not be manifested; neither was any thing kept secret, but that it should come abroad. If any man have ears to hear, let him hear.

And he said unto them, Take heed what ye hear: with what measure ye mete, it shall be measured to you: and unto you that hear shall more be given. For he that hath, to him shall be given: and he that hath not, from him shall be taken even that which he hath.

Amp—Those that were sown on the good (well-adapted) soil are the ones who hear the Word, and receive and accept and welcome it and bear fruit, some thirty times as much as was sown, some sixty times as much, and some [even] a hundred times as much. And He said to them, Is the lamp brought in to be put under a peck-measure, or under a bed, and not on the [lamp] stand? Things are hidden [temporarily] only as a means to revelation. For there is nothing hidden except to be revealed, nor is anything [temporarily] kept secret except in order that it may be made known. If any man has ears to hear, let him be listening, and perceive and comprehend.

And He said to them, Be careful what you are hearing. The measure [of thought and study] you give [to the truth you hear] will be the measure [of virtue and knowledge] that comes back to you, and more [besides] will be given to you who hear. For to him who has will more be given, and from him who has nothing, even what he has will be taken away (by force).

Moffatt—"As for those who were sown 'on good soil,' these are the people who listen to the word and take it in, bearing fruit at the rate of thirty, sixty, and a hundredfold." He also said to them, "Is a lamp brought to be placed under a bowl or a bed? Is it not to be placed upon the stand? Nothing is hidden except to be disclosed, nothing concealed except to be revealed. If anyone has an ear to hear, let him listen to this."

Also he said to them, "Take care what you hear; the measure you deal out to others will be dealt out to yourselves, and you will receive extra. For he who has, to him shall more be given; while as for him who has not, from him shall be taken even what he has."

NIV—"Others, like seed sown on good soil, hear the word, accept it, and produce a crop—thirty, sixty or even a hundred times what was sown." He said to them, "Do you bring in a lamp to put it under a bowl or a bed? Instead, don't you put it on its stand? For whatever is hidden is meant to be disclosed, and whatever is concealed is meant to be brought out into the open. If anyone has ears to hear, let him hear."

"Consider carefully what you hear," he continued. "With the measure you use, it will be measured to you—and even more. Whoever has will be given more; whoever does not have, even what he has will be taken from him."

*Prosperity
Promises*

Mark 10:17-21

KJV—And when he was gone forth into the way, there came one running, and kneeled to him, and asked him, Good Master, what shall I do that I may inherit eternal life? And Jesus said unto him, Why callest thou me good? there is none good but one, that is, God. Thou knowest the commandments, Do not commit adultery, Do not kill, Do not steal, Do not bear false witness, Defraud not, Honour thy father and mother.

And he answered and said unto him, Master, all these have I observed from my youth. Then Jesus beholding him loved him, and said unto him, One thing thou lackest: go thy way, sell whatsoever thou hast, and give to the poor, and thou shalt have treasure in heaven: and come, take up the cross, and follow me.

Amp—And as He was setting out on His journey, a man ran up and knelt before Him, and asked Him, Teacher, (You are essentially and perfectly morally) good, what must I do to inherit eternal life (that is, to partake of eternal salvation in the Messiah's kingdom)? And Jesus said to him, Why do you call Me (essentially and perfectly morally) good? There is no one (essentially and perfectly morally) good except God alone. You know the commandments: Do not kill; do not commit adultery; do not steal; do not bear false witness; do not defraud; honor your father and mother.

And he replied to Him, Teacher, I have carefully guarded and observed all these and taken care not to violate them from my boyhood. And Jesus looking upon him loved him, and He said to him, You lack one thing; go and sell all you have, and give [the money] to the poor, and you will have treasure in heaven; and come [and] accompany Me—walking the same road that I walk.

Moffatt—As he went out on the road, a man ran up and knelt down before him. "Good teacher," he asked, "what must I do to inherit life eternal?" Jesus said to him, "Why call me 'good'? No one is good, no one but God. You know the commandments: do not kill, do not commit adultery, do not steal, do not bear false witness, do not defraud, honour your father and mother."

"Teacher," he said, "I have observed all these commands from my youth." Jesus looked at him and loved him. "There is one thing you want," he said; "go and sell all you have; give the money to the poor and you will have treasure in heaven; then come, take up the cross, and follow me."

NIV—As Jesus started on his way, a man ran up to him and fell on his knees before him. "Good teacher," he asked, "what must I do to inherit eternal life?" "Why do you call me good?" Jesus answered. "No one is good—except God alone. You know the commandments: 'Do not murder, do not commit adultery, do not steal, do not give false testimony, do not defraud, honor your father and mother.'"

"Teacher," he declared, "all these I have kept since I was a boy." Jesus looked at him and loved him. "One thing you lack," he said. "Go, sell everything you have and give to the poor, and you will have treasure in heaven. Then come, follow me."

Mark 10:29-30

KJV—Jesus answered and said, Verily I say unto you, There is no man that hath left house, or brethren, or sisters, or father, or mother, or wife, or children, or lands, for my sake, and the gospel's, But he shall receive an hundredfold now in this time, houses, and brethren, and sisters, and mothers, and children, and lands, with persecutions; and in the world to come eternal life.

Amp—Jesus said, Truly, I tell you, there is no one who has given up and left house or brothers or sisters or mother or father or children or lands, for My sake and for the Gospel, Who will not receive a hundred times as much now in this time, houses and brothers and sisters and mothers and children and lands, with persecutions, and in the age to come eternal life.

Moffatt—Jesus said, "I tell you truly, no one has left home or brothers or sisters or mother or father or children or lands for my sake and for the sake of the gospel, who does not get a hundred times as much—in this present world homes, brothers, sisters, mothers, children and lands, together with persecutions, and in the world to come life eternal."

NIV— "I tell you the truth," Jesus replied, "no one who has left home or brothers or sisters or mother or father or children or fields for me and the gospel will fail to receive a hundred times as much in this present age (homes, brothers, sisters, mothers, children and fields—and with them, persecutions) and in the age to come, eternal life."

Luke 6:38

KJV—Give, and it shall be given unto you; good measure, pressed down, and shaken together, and running over, shall men give into your bosom. For with the same measure that ye mete withal it shall be measured to you again.

Amp—Give, and [gifts] will be given you, good measure, pressed down, shaken together and running over will they pour into [the pouch formed by] the bosom [of your robe and used as a bag]. For with the measure you deal out—that is, with the measure you use when you confer benefits on others—it will be measured back to you.

Moffatt—Give, and you will have ample measure given you—they will pour into your lap measure pressed down, shaken together, and running over; for the measure you deal out to others will be dealt back to yourselves.

NIV—Give, and it will be given to you. A good measure, pressed down, shaken together and running over, will be poured into your lap. For with the measure you use, it will be measured to you.

Luke 7:23

KJV—Blessed is he, whosoever shall not be offended in me.

Amp—Blessed—happy [with life-joy and satisfaction in God's favor and salvation apart from outward conditions] and to be envied—is he who takes no offense in Me and who is not hurt or resentful or annoyed or repelled or made to stumble, [whatever may occur].

Moffatt—Blessed is he who is repelled by nothing in me!

NIV—Blessed is the man who does not fall away on account of me.

Luke 12:16-21

KJV—The ground of a certain rich man brought forth plentifully: And he thought within himself, saying, What shall I do, because I have no room where to bestow my fruits? And he said, This will I do: I will pull down my barns, and build greater; and there will I bestow all my fruits and my goods. And I will say to my soul, Soul, thou hast much goods laid up for many years; take thine ease, eat, drink, and be merry. But God said unto him, Thou fool, this night thy soul shall be required of thee: then whose shall those things be, which thou hast provided? So is he that layeth up treasure for himself, and is not rich toward God.

Amp—The land of a rich man was very fertile and yielded plentifully; And he considered and debated within himself, What shall I do? I have no place to gather together my harvest. And he said, I will do this: I will pull down my storehouses and build larger ones; and there I will store all my grain (produce) and my goods. And I will say to my soul, Soul, you have many good things laid up, [enough] for many years, take your ease, eat, drink and enjoy yourself merrily. But God said to him, You fool! This very night they [that is, the messengers of God] demand your soul of you; and all the things that you have prepared, whose will they be? So it is with him who continues to lay up and hoard possessions for himself, and is not rich [in his relation] to God—this is how he fares.

Moffatt—A rich man's estate bore heavy crops. So he debated, "What am I to do? I have no room to store my crops." And he said, "This is what I will do. I will pull down my granaries and build larger ones, where I can store all my produce and my goods. And I will say to my soul, 'Soul, you have ample stores laid up for many a year; take your ease, eat, drink and be merry.'" But God said to him, "Foolish man, this very night your soul is required from you; and who will get all you have prepared?" So fares the man who lays up treasure for himself, instead of gaining the riches of God.

NIV—The ground of a certain rich man produced a good crop. He thought to himself, "What shall I do? I have no place to store my crops." Then he said, "This is what

I'll do. I will tear down my barns and build bigger ones, and there I will store all my grain and my goods. And I'll say to myself, 'You have plenty of good things laid up for many years. Take life easy; eat, drink and be merry.'" But God said to him, "You fool! This very night your life will be demanded from you. Then who will get what you have prepared for yourself?" This is how it will be with anyone who stores up things for himself but is not rich toward God.

Luke 12:32-33

KJV—Fear not, little flock; for it is your Father's good pleasure to give you the kingdom. Sell that ye have, and give alms; provide yourselves bags which wax not old, a treasure in the heavens that faileth not, where no thief approacheth, neither moth corrupteth.

Amp—Do not be seized with alarm and struck with fear, little flock, for it is your Father's good pleasure to give you the kingdom! Sell what you possess and give donations to the poor; provide yourselves with purses and handbags that do not grow old, an unfailing and inexhaustible treasure in the heavens, where no thief comes near and no moth destroys.

Moffatt—Fear not, you little flock, for your Father's delight is to give you the Realm. Sell what you possess and give it away in alms, make purses for yourselves that never wear out: get treasure in heaven that never fails, that no thief can get at, no moth destroy.

NIV—Do not be afraid, little flock, for your Father has been pleased to give you the kingdom. Sell your possessions and give to the poor. Provide purses for yourselves that will not wear out, a treasure in heaven that will not be exhausted, where no thief comes near and no moth destroys.

Luke 12:42-44

KJV—The Lord said, Who then is that faithful and wise steward, whom his lord shall make ruler over his household, to give them their portion of meat in due season? Blessed is that servant, whom his lord when he cometh shall find so doing. Of a truth I say unto you, that he will make him ruler over all that he hath.

Amp—The Lord said, Who then is that faithful steward, the wise man whom his master will set over those in his household service, to supply them their allowance of food at the appointed time? Blessed— happy, and to be envied—is that servant whom his master finds so doing when he arrives. Truly, I tell you, he will set him in charge over all his possessions.

Moffatt—The Lord said, "Well, where is the trusty, thoughtful steward whom the lord and master will set over his establishment, to give out supplies at the proper time? Blessed is that servant if his lord and master finds him so doing when he arrives! I tell you plainly, he will set him over all his property."

NIV—The Lord answered, "Who then is the faithful and wise manager, whom the master puts in charge of his servants to give them their food allowance at the proper time? It will be good for that servant whom the master finds doing so when he returns. I tell you the truth, he will put him in charge of all his possessions."

Luke 16:10-12

KJV—He that is faithful in that which is least is faithful also in much: and he that is unjust in the least is unjust also in much. If therefore ye have not been faithful in the unrighteous mammon, who will commit to your trust the true riches? And if ye have not been faithful in that which is another man's, who shall give you that which is your own?

Amp—He who is faithful in a very little [thing], is faithful also in much; and he who is dishonest and unjust in a very little [thing], is dishonest and unjust also in much. Therefore, if you have not been faithful in the [case of] the unrighteous mammon—the deceitful riches, money, possessions—who will entrust to you the true riches? And if you have not proved faithful in that which belongs to another [whether God or man], who will give you that which is your own [that is, the true riches]?

Moffatt—He who is faithful with a trifle is also faithful with a large trust, and he who is dishonest with a trifle is also dishonest with a large trust. So if you are not faithful with dishonest mammon, how can you ever be trusted with true Riches? And if you are not faithful with what belongs to another, how can you ever be given what is your own?

NIV—Whoever can be trusted with very little can also be trusted with much, and whoever is dishonest with very little will also be dishonest with much. So if you have not been trustworthy in handling worldly wealth, who will trust you with true riches? And if you have not been trustworthy with someone else's property, who will give you property of your own?

John 10:10

KJV—The thief cometh not, but for to steal, and to kill, and to destroy: I am come that they might have life, and that they might have it more abundantly.

Amp—The thief comes only in order that he may steal and may kill and may destroy. I came that they may have and enjoy life, and have it in abundance—to the full, till it overflows.

Moffatt—The thief only comes to steal, to slay, and to destroy: I have come that they may have life and have it to the full.

NIV—The thief comes only to steal and kill and destroy; I have come that they may have life, and have it to the full.

John 16:23-24

KJV—In that day ye shall ask me nothing. Verily, verily, I say unto you, Whatsoever ye shall ask the Father in my name, he will give it you. Hitherto have ye asked nothing in my name: ask, and ye shall receive, that your joy may be full.

Amp—When that time comes, you will ask nothing of Me—you will need to ask Me no questions. I assure you, most solemnly I tell you, that My Father will grant you whatever you ask in My name [presenting all I AM]. Up to this time, you have not asked a [single] thing in My name [that is, presenting all I AM] but now ask and keep on asking and you will receive, so that your joy (gladness, delight) may be full and complete.

Moffatt—On that day you will not ask me any questions. Truly, truly I tell you, whatever you ask the Father, he will give you in my name; hitherto you have asked nothing in my name; ask and you will receive, that your joy may be full.

NIV—In that day you will no longer ask me anything. I tell you the truth, my Father will give you whatever you ask in my name. Until now you have not asked for anything in my name. Ask and you will receive, and your joy will be complete.

The End~Time
Transfer of Wealth

As you study the subject of prosperity, it becomes clear that God is a God of justice as well as mercy. He is fair in all His dealings. In His Word, He has given clear instruction of how to live a godly life, which is the foundation for prosperity. When we are obedient to follow His ways, He will take care of us and bless us. But those who refuse to go God's way will have a different outcome. Psalm 37:28 in *The Amplified Bible* says, "*The Lord delights in justice and forsakes not His saints; they are preserved for ever, but the offspring of the wicked [in time] shall be cut off.*" And Proverbs 28:8 says, "*He who by charging excessive interest and by unjust efforts to get gain increases his material possession, gathers it for him [to spend] who is kind and generous to the poor.*" It is an immutable law that one cannot truly prosper in all areas of life if he does not serve and obey God (see Deuteronomy 28:15-68). God prospers those who love and obey Him.

Some people may feel that God is taking a long time to fulfill some of His promises, but 2 Peter 3:9 says, "The Lord does not delay and be tardy or slow about what He promises, according to some people's conception of slowness, but He is long-suffering (extraordinarily patient) toward you, not desiring that any should perish, but that all should turn to repentance" (The Amplified Bible). God is giving the unrighteous plenty of time to repent, however, He is well aware of what they are doing in the meantime (Proverbs 5:21, 15:3). They may appear to prosper through evildoing, but their success will be short-lived (James 5:1-4; Psalm 37:7-9). The Word of God indicates that in the last days, there will be a transfer of wealth from the hands of the wicked to the hands of the just. God is actually giving sinners the job of storing up wealth for the righteous (Ecclesiastes 2:26).

That wealth can come into the kingdom of God in different ways. There are those who receive Jesus as their Lord and Savior and bring their resources with them. This is really what God wants for all sinners—to have them become a part of the family of God. Then they can become partakers of the blessings of God.

Another way the wealth can be transferred is through faith and the Word of God operating in believers' lives—such as through the hundredfold return. People who are increasing their giving as they grow will see ever-increasing returns on their giving—as the reservoirs that have held riches from unjust gain are tapped. The wicked rich who refuse to obey God will begin to see their wealth dwindle. Riches will return to the hands of the givers.

So learn to give. Get your words in line with God's Word. Believe for the hundred-fold return—and for the wealth of the wicked to come into your hands, because *"The wealth of the sinner is laid up for the just"* (Proverbs 13:22).

James 5:1-4

KJV—Go to now, ye rich men, weep and howl for your miseries that shall come upon you. Your riches are corrupted, and your garments are motheaten. Your gold and silver is cankered; and the rust of them shall be a witness against you, and shall eat your flesh as it were fire. Ye have heaped treasure together for the last days.

Behold, the hire of the labourers who have reaped down your fields, which is of you kept back by fraud, crieth: and the cries of them which have reaped are entered into the ears of the Lord of sabaoth.

Amp—Come now, you rich [people], weep aloud and lament over the miseries—the woes—that are surely coming upon you. Your abundant wealth has rotted and is ruined and your [many] garments have become moth-eaten. Your gold and silver are completely rusted through, and their rust will be testimony against you and it will devour your flesh as if it were fire. You have heaped together treasure for the last days.

[But] look! [Here are] the wages that you have withheld by fraud from the laborers who have reaped your fields, crying out (for vengeance), and the cries of the harvesters have come to the ears of the Lord of hosts.

Moffatt—Come now, you rich men, weep and shriek over your impending miseries! You have been storing up treasure in the very last days; your wealth lies rotting, and your clothes are moth-eaten; your gold and silver lie rusted over, and their rust will be evidence against you, it will devour your flesh like fire.

See, the wages of which you have defrauded the workmen who mowed your fields call out, and the cries of the harvesters have reached the ears of the Lord of Hosts.

NIV—Now listen, you rich people, weep and wail because of the misery that is coming upon you. Your wealth has rotted, and moths have eaten your clothes. Your gold and silver are corroded. Their corrosion will testify against you and eat your flesh like fire. You have hoarded wealth in the last days.

Look! The wages you failed to pay the workmen who mowed your fields are crying out against you. The cries of the harvesters have reached the ears of the Lord Almighty.

Here are some promises that you, as a child of God, can stand on regarding the transfer of wealth in these last days.

Job 27:13-17

KJV—This is the portion of a wicked man with God, and the heritage of oppressors, which they shall receive of the Almighty.... Though he heap up silver as the dust, and prepare raiment as the clay; He may prepare it, but the just shall put it on, and the innocent shall divide the silver.

Amp—This [I am about to tell] is the portion of a wicked man with God, and the heritage which oppressors shall receive from the Almighty.... Though he heaps up silver like dust, and piles up clothing like clay; He may prepare it, but the just will wear it, and the innocent will divide the silver.

Moffatt—Here is what God awards an evil man, what the Almighty bestows upon a tyrant...he may store silver up like dust, and prepare robes abundant as the clay; he may prepare them, but the just shall wear them, and good men shall divide his silver.

NIV—Here is the fate God allots to the wicked, the heritage a ruthless man receives from the Almighty.... Though he heaps up silver like dust and clothes like piles of clay, what he lays up the righteous will wear, and the innocent will divide his silver.

234

*Prosperity
Promises*

Psalm 37:7-11, 28-29

KJV—Rest in the Lord, and wait patiently for him: fret not thyself because of him who prospereth in his way, because of the man who bringeth wicked devices to pass....

For evildoers shall be cut off: but those that wait upon the Lord, they shall inherit the earth. For yet a little while, and the wicked shall not be: yea, thou shalt diligently consider his place, and it shall not be. But the meek shall inherit the earth; and shall delight themselves in the abundance of peace....

For the Lord loveth judgment, and forsaketh not his saints; they are preserved for ever: but the seed of the wicked shall be cut off. The righteous shall inherit the land, and dwell therein for ever.

Amp—Be still and rest in the Lord; wait for Him, and patiently stay yourself upon Him;

fret not yourself because of him who prospers in his way, because of the man who brings wicked devices to pass....

For evildoers shall be cut off; but those who wait and hope and look for the Lord, [in the end] shall inherit the earth. For yet a little while and the evildoer will be no more; though you look with care where he used to be, he will not be found. But the meek [in the end] shall inherit the earth, and shall delight themselves in the abundance of peace....

For the Lord delights in justice and forsakes not His saints; they are preserved for ever, but the offspring of the wicked [in time] shall be cut off. [Then] the [consistently] righteous shall inherit the land, and dwell upon it for ever.

Moffatt—Leave it to the Eternal and be patient; fret not over the successful man, who aims to slay the upright, and carries out his wicked plan....

Evildoers shall indeed be rooted out, and the land left to those who wait for the Eternal. A little longer, and the godless will be gone; look in his haunts, and he is there no more! The land will be left to the humble, to enjoy plenteous prosperity...for the Eternal, who loves honesty, never forsakes his faithful band. The lawless shall be utterly destroyed...the land is the possession of the good, and all their days they shall dwell there.

NIV—Be still before the Lord and wait patiently for him; do not fret when men succeed in their ways, when they carry out their wicked schemes....

For evil men will be cut off, but those who hope in the Lord will inherit the land. A little while, and the wicked will be no more; though you look for them, they will not be found. But the meek will inherit the land and enjoy great peace....

For the Lord loves the just and will not forsake his faithful ones. They will be protected forever, but the offspring of the wicked will be cut off; the righteous will inherit the land and dwell in it forever.

Proverbs 13:22

KJV—The wealth of the sinner is laid up for the just.

Amp—The wealth of the sinner [finds its way eventually] into the hands of the righteous, for whom it was laid up.

Moffatt—The sinner lays up treasure—to enrich the good!

NIV—A sinner's wealth is stored up for the righteous.

Proverbs 28:8

KJV—He that by usury and unjust gain increaseth his substance, he shall gather it for him that will pity the poor.

Amp—He who by charging excessive interest and by unjust efforts to get gain increases his material possession, gathers it for him [to spend] who is kind and generous to the poor.

Moffatt—He who adds to his income by taking interest will lose his money to some charitable soul.

NIV—He who increases his wealth by exorbitant interest amasses it for another, who will be kind to the poor.

Ecclesiastes 2:26

KJV—For God giveth to a man that is good in his sight wisdom, and knowledge, and joy: but to the sinner he giveth travail, to gather and to heap up, that he may give to him that is good before God.

Amp—For to the person who pleases Him God gives wisdom and knowledge and joy; but to the sinner He gives the work of gathering and heaping up, that he may give to one who pleases God.

Moffatt—To a man whom God approves, he grants wisdom, knowledge, and happiness, but he sets a sinner the task of gathering and amassing wealth, only to leave it to the man whom God approves.

NIV—To the man who pleases him, God gives wisdom, knowledge and happiness, but to the sinner he gives the task of gathering and storing up wealth to hand it over to the one who pleases God.

Isaiah 60

KJV—Arise, shine; for thy light is come, and the glory of the Lord is risen upon thee. For, behold, the darkness shall cover the earth, and gross darkness the people: but the Lord shall arise upon thee, and his glory shall be seen upon thee. And the Gentiles shall come to thy light, and kings to the brightness of thy rising.

Lift up thine eyes round about, and see: all they gather themselves together, they come to thee: thy sons shall come from far, and thy daughters shall be nursed at thy side. Then thou shalt see, and flow together, and thine heart shall fear, and be enlarged; because the abundance of the sea shall be converted unto thee, the forces of the Gentiles shall come unto thee.

The multitude of camels shall cover thee, the dromedaries of Midian and Ephah; all they from Sheba shall come: they shall bring gold and incense; and they shall show forth the praises of the Lord. All the flocks of Kedar shall be gathered together unto thee, the rams of Nebaioth shall minister unto thee: they shall come up with acceptance on mine altar, and I will glorify the house of my glory.

Who are these that fly as a cloud, and as the doves to their windows? Surely the isles shall wait for me, and the ships of Tarshish first, to bring thy sons from far, their silver and their gold with them, unto the name of the Lord thy God, and to the Holy One of Israel, because he hath glorified thee.

And the sons of strangers shall build up thy walls, and their kings shall minister unto thee: for in my wrath I smote thee, but in my favour have I had mercy on thee. Therefore thy gates shall be open continually; they shall not be shut day nor night; that men may bring unto thee the forces of the Gentiles, and that their kings may be brought.

For the nation and kingdom that will not serve thee shall perish; yea, those nations shall be utterly wasted. The glory of Lebanon shall come unto thee, the fir tree, the pine tree, and the box together, to beautify the place of my sanctuary; and I will make the place of my feet glorious.

The sons also of them that afflicted thee shall come bending unto thee; and all they that despised thee shall bow themselves down at the soles of thy feet; and they shall call thee, The city of the Lord, The Zion of the Holy One of Israel. Whereas thou hast been forsaken and hated, so that no man went through thee, I will make thee an eternal excellency, a joy of many generations.

Thou shalt also suck the milk of the Gentiles, and shalt suck the breast of kings: and thou shalt know that I the Lord am thy Saviour and thy Redeemer, the mighty One of Jacob. For brass I will bring gold, and for iron I will bring silver, and for wood brass, and for stones iron: I will also make thy officers peace, and thine exactors righteousness.

Violence shall no more be heard in thy land, wasting nor destruction within thy borders; but thou shalt call thy walls Salvation, and thy gates Praise. The sun shall be no more thy light by day; neither for brightness shall the moon give light unto thee: but the Lord shall be unto thee an everlasting light, and thy God thy glory.

Thy sun shall no more go down; neither shall thy moon withdraw itself: for the Lord shall be thine everlasting light, and the days of thy mourning shall be ended. Thy people also shall be all righteous: they shall inherit the land for ever, the branch of my planting, the work of my hands, that I may be glorified. A little one shall become a thousand, and a small one a strong nation: I the Lord will hasten it in his time.

NIV—Arise, shine, for your light has come, and the glory of the Lord rises upon you. See, darkness covers the earth and thick darkness is over the peoples, but the Lord rises upon you and his glory appears over you. Nations will come to your light, and kings to the brightness of your dawn.

Lift up your eyes and look about you: All assemble and come to you; your sons come from afar, and your daughters are carried on the arm. Then you will look and be radiant, your heart will throb and swell with joy; the wealth on the seas will be brought to you, to you the riches of the nations will come.

Herds of camels will cover your land, young camels of Midian and Ephah. And all from Sheba will come, bearing gold and incense and proclaiming the praise of the Lord. All Kedar's flocks will be gathered to you, the rams of Nebaioth will serve you; they will be accepted as offerings on my altar, and I will adorn my glorious temple.

Who are these that fly along like clouds, like doves to their nests? Surely the islands look to me; in the lead are the ships of Tarshish, bringing your sons from afar, with their silver and gold, to the honor of the Lord your God, the Holy One of Israel, for he has endowed you with splendor.

Foreigners will rebuild your walls, and their kings will serve you. Though in anger I struck you, in favor I will show you compassion.

*The End-Time
Transfer
of Wealth*

Your gates will always stand open, they will never be shut, day or night, so that men may bring you the wealth of the nations—their kings led in triumphal procession.

For the nation or kingdom that will not serve you will perish; it will be utterly ruined. The glory of Lebanon will come to you, the pine, the fir and the cypress together, to adorn the place of my sanctuary; and I will glorify the place of my feet.

The sons of your oppressors will come bowing before you; all who despise you will bow down at your feet and will call you the City of the Lord, Zion of the Holy One of Israel. Although you have been forsaken and hated, with no one traveling through, I will make you the everlasting pride and the joy of all generations.

You will drink the milk of nations and be nursed at royal breasts. Then you will know that I, the Lord, am your Savior, your Redeemer, the Mighty One of Jacob. Instead of bronze I will bring you gold, and silver in place of iron. Instead of wood I will bring you bronze, and iron in place of stones. I will make peace your governor and righteousness your ruler.

No longer will violence be heard in your land, nor ruin or destruction within your borders, but you will call your walls Salvation and your gates Praise. The sun will no more be your light by day, nor will the brightness of the moon shine on you, for the Lord will be your everlasting light, and your God will be your glory.

Your sun will never set again, and your moon will wane no more; the Lord will be your everlasting light, and your days of sorrow will end. Then will all your people be righteous and they will possess the land forever. They are the shoot I have planted, the work of my hands, for the display of my splendor. The least of you will become a thousand, the smallest a mighty nation. I am the Lord; in its time I will do this swiftly.

Haggai 2:7-9

KJV—I will shake all nations, and the desire of all nations shall come: and I will fill this house with glory, saith the Lord of hosts. The silver is mine, and the gold is mine, saith the Lord of hosts. The glory of this latter house shall be greater than of the former, saith the Lord of hosts: and in this place will I give peace, saith the Lord of hosts.

Amp—I will shake all nations, and the desire and the precious things of all nations shall come in, and I will fill this house with splendor, says the Lord of hosts. The silver is Mine, and the gold is Mine, says the Lord of hosts. The latter glory of this house [with its successor, to which Jesus came] shall be greater than the former, says the Lord of hosts; and in this place will I give peace and prosperity, says the Lord of hosts.

Moffatt—Shaking all nations till the treasures of all nations are brought hither and my House here filled with splendour (says the Lord of hosts). Mine is the silver, mine the gold, the Lord of hosts declares; the later splendour of this House shall outshine the former (says the Lord of hosts), and I will make this place prosper, says the Lord of hosts.

NIV—"I will shake all nations, and the desired of all nations will come, and I will fill this house with glory," says the Lord Almighty. "The silver is mine and the gold is mine," declares the Lord Almighty. "The glory of this present house will be greater than the glory of the former house," says the Lord Almighty. "And in this place I will grant peace," declares the Lord Almighty.

Ephesians 3:20

KJV—Now unto him that is able to do exceeding abundantly above all that we ask or think, according to the power that worketh in us.

Amp—Now to Him Who, by (in consequence of) the [action of His] power that is at work within us, is able to [carry out His purpose and] do superabundantly, far over

and above all that we [dare] ask or think—
infinitely beyond our highest prayers, desires, thoughts, hopes or dreams.

Moffatt—Now to him who by the action of
his power within us is able to do all, aye far
more than we can ever ask or imagine.

NIV—Now to him who is able to do immeasurably more than all we ask or imagine, according to his power that is at work
within us.

**In 1978, Brother Charles Capps
delivered the following prophecy about
the end-time transfer of wealth.
It confirms the Scripture and God's plan
for the Church in the end times.**

Financial inversion shall increase in
these days. For you see, it is My desire
to move in the realm of your financial
prosperity. But release Me, saith the
Lord, release Me that I may come in
your behalf and move on your behalf.

For yes, yes, yes, there shall be in
this hour financial distress here and
there. The economy shall go up and it
will go down; but those that learn to
walk in the Word, they shall see the
PROSPERITY OF THE WORD come
forth in this hour in a way that has not
been seen by men in days past.

Yes, there's coming a FINANCIAL IN-VERSION in the world's system. It's been held in reservoirs of wicked men for days on end. But the end is nigh. Those reservoirs shall be tapped and shall be drained into the gospel of Jesus Christ. It shall be done, saith the Lord. It shall be done IN THE TIME ALLOTTED and so shall it be that the Word of the Lord shall come to pass that the wealth of the sinner is laid up for the just.

Predominantly in two ways shall it be done in this hour. Those that have hoarded up and stored because of the inspiration of the evil one and held the money from the gospel shall be con-verted and drawn into the kingdom and then shall it release that reservoir into the kingdom. But many, many will not. They'll not heed the voice of the Word of God. They'll turn aside to this and they'll turn to that and they'll walk in their own ways, but their ways will not work in this hour. It'll dwindle and it'll slip away as though it were in bags with holes in them. It'll go here and it'll go there and they'll wonder why it's not working now. "It worked in days past," they'll say.

But it shall be, saith the Lord, that THE WORD OF THE LORD SHALL RISE WITHIN MEN—men of God of low esteem in the financial world—that shall claim the Word of God to be their very own and walk in the light of it as it has been set forth in the Word and give. They'll begin to give small at first because that's all they have, but then it will increase, and THROUGH THE HUNDREDFOLD RETURN, so shall it be that the reservoirs that have held the riches in days past, so shall it return to the hands of the giver. BECAUSE OF THE HUNDREDFOLD RETURN SHALL THE RESERVOIRS BE LOST FROM THE WICKED AND TURNED TO THE GOSPEL. For it shall be, it shall be in this hour that you will see things that you've never dreamed come to pass. Oh, it'll be strong at first in ways, then it will grow greater and greater until men will be astounded and the world will stand in awe because the ways of men have failed and the ways of God shall come forth.

As men walk in My Word, so shall they walk in the ways of the Lord. Oh yes, there will be some who say, "Yes, but God's ways are higher, surely higher than our ways, and we can't walk in those." It's true that the ways of God are higher. They are higher than your ways as the heavens are above the earth, but I'll teach you to walk in My ways. I never did say you couldn't walk in My ways. Now learn to walk in it. Learn to give. So shall the inversion of the financial system revert and so shall it be that the gospel of the kingdom shall be preached to all the world, and THERE SHALL BE NO LACK IN THE KINGDOM. Those that give shall walk in the ways of the supernatural! They shall be known abroad. MY WORD SHALL SPREAD AND THE KNOWLEDGE OF THE LORD SHALL FILL ALL THE EARTH IN THE DAY AND THE HOUR IN WHICH YE STAND. Ye shall see it and know it for it is of Me and it shall come to pass, saith the Lord.

Chapter 9

Confess
Prosperity

God created all things by the power of His Word. Each time God spoke, He released His own faith—which was the very creative power that brought His words to pass.

Words. They are spiritual containers that carry the power to shape our destiny. Our words contain and release our faith. But what is most exciting is that when we speak God's words about our lives, we release the creative power of God's faith into our situations.

When you speak the Word of God out of your mouth, it is as much the Word of God and has the same authority as when God personally said, "Let there be light" (Genesis 1:3).

I can't tell you how many times we have found this to be true in our own lives. Any time we have attacked our lack in an area with God's creative words of increase and abundance, provision was there for us—every time. And I want you to know, having God speak in your behalf makes a tremendous difference in the outcome. Circumstances are subject to change. God's Word never changes.

Just as confession is made *unto* salvation, confession is also made *unto* prosperity or *unto* healing or *unto whatever* it is we need from God. By meditating on the Word, we become persuaded of God's promises and confident in His willingness to perform those promises in our lives. That's exactly what real faith is—being persuaded and confident that God will do for us just what He said He'd do.

So, every time we confess the Word of God from a heart that's confident God will do in our lives what He said—according to Jesus in Mark 11:24—we shall have what we say.

Joshua 1:8

KJV—This book of the law shall not depart out of thy mouth; but thou shalt meditate therein day and night, that thou mayest observe to do according to all that is written therein: for then thou shalt make thy way prosperous, and then thou shalt have good success.

Amp—This book of the law shall not depart out of your mouth, but you shall meditate on it day and night, that you may observe and do according to all that is written in it; for then you shall make your way prosperous, and then you shall deal wisely and have good success.

Moffatt—This lawbook you shall never cease to have on your lips; you must pore over it day and night, that you may be mindful to carry out all that is written in it, for so shall you make your way prosperous, so shall you succeed.

NIV—Do not let this Book of the Law depart from your mouth; meditate on it day and night, so that you may be careful to do everything written in it. Then you will be prosperous and successful.

Matthew 12:34-37

KJV—Out of the abundance of the heart the mouth speaketh. A good man out of the good treasure of the heart bringeth forth good things: and an evil man out of the evil treasure bringeth forth evil things. But I say unto you, That every idle word that men shall speak, they shall give account thereof in the day of judgment. For by thy words thou shalt be justified, and by thy words thou shalt be condemned.

Amp—Out of the fullness—the overflow, the superabundance—of the heart the mouth speaks. The good man from his inner good treasure flings forth good things, and the evil man out of his inner evil storehouse flings forth evil things. But I tell you, on the day of judgment men will have to give account for every idle (inoperative, non-working) word they speak. For by your words you will be justified and acquitted, and by your words you will be condemned and sentenced.

Moffatt—The mouth utters what the heart is full of. The good man brings good out of his good store, and the evil man brings evil out of his store of evil. I tell you, on the day of judgment men will have to account for every careless word they utter; for by your words you will be acquitted, and by your words you will be condemned.

NIV—Out of the overflow of the heart the mouth speaks. The good man brings good things out of the good stored up in him, and the evil man brings evil things out of the evil stored up in him. But I tell you that men will have to give account on the day of judgment for every careless word they have spoken. For by your words you will be acquitted, and by your words you will be condemned.

Mark 11:23

KJV—For verily I say unto you, That whosoever shall say unto this mountain, Be thou removed, and be thou cast into the sea; and shall not doubt in his heart, but shall believe that those things which he saith shall come to pass; he shall have whatsoever he saith.

Amp—Truly, I tell you, whoever says to this mountain, Be lifted up and thrown into the sea! and does not doubt at all in his heart, but believes that what he says will take place, it will be done for him.

Confess Prosperity

Moffatt—I tell you truly, whoever says to this hill, "Take and throw yourself into the sea," and has not a doubt in his mind but believes that what he says will happen, he will have it done.

NIV—I tell you the truth, if anyone says to this mountain, "Go, throw yourself into the sea," and does not doubt in his heart but believes that what he says will happen, it will be done for him.

Hebrews 4:12

KJV—For the word of God is quick, and powerful, and sharper than any twoedged sword, piercing even to the dividing asunder

of soul and spirit, and of the joints and marrow, and is a discerner of the thoughts and
intents of the heart.

Amp—For the Word that God speaks is
alive and full of power—making it active,
operative, energizing and effective; it is
sharper than any two-edged sword, penetrating to the dividing line of the breath of
life (soul) and [the immortal] spirit, and of
joints and marrow [that is, of the deepest
parts of our nature] exposing and sifting
and analyzing and judging the very
thoughts and purposes of the heart.

Moffatt—For the Logos of God is a living
thing, active and more cutting than any
sword with double edge, penetrating to the
very division of soul and spirit, joints and
marrow—scrutinizing the very thoughts and
conceptions of the heart.

NIV—For the word of God is living and
active. Sharper than any double-edged
sword, it penetrates even to dividing soul
and spirit, joints and marrow; it judges the
thoughts and attitudes of the heart.

Prosperity Confessions

*Speak God's powerful, active, liv-
ing Word over all the situations in
your life, including your prosperity.*

Many of the scriptures in this book need to become part of your daily confession of faith for yourself and your household.

God wants His people to receive everything He has promised, and knowing what He promised is vital. So read and meditate on the promises throughout these pages, and remember that God's will is always to prosper His people—He will never forget you nor forsake you!

Christ has redeemed me from the curse of the law. Christ has redeemed me from poverty; Christ has redeemed me from sickness; Christ has redeemed me from spiritual death (Galatians 3:13-14; Deuteronomy 28).

Jesus has delivered me from poverty and given me wealth. He set me free from sickness and has given me health. He has delivered me from spiritual death and has given me eternal life (2 Corinthians 8:9; Isaiah 53:5-6; John 10:10, 5:24).

God is able to make all grace (every favor and earthly blessing) come to me in abundance, so that I may always and under all circumstances and whatever the need, be self-sufficient—possessing enough to require no aid or support and furnished in abundance for every good work and charitable donation....

Thus I will be enriched in all things and in every way, so that I can be generous, [and my generosity as it is] administered...will bring forth thanksgiving to God (2 Corinthians 9:8, 11, *The Amplified Bible*).

I delight myself in the Lord and He gives me the desires of my heart (Psalm 37:4).

I have given and it is given to me good measure, pressed down, shaken together, running over. Men give me—all the time (Luke 6:38).

With the measure I mete, it is measured to me. I sow bountifully therefore I reap bountifully. I give cheerfully, and my God has made all grace abound toward me. Having all sufficiency of all things, I do abound to all good works (2 Corinthians 9:6-8).

I do not lack any good thing, for my God supplies all of my need according to His riches in glory by Christ Jesus (Philippians 4:19).

The Lord is my shepherd and I DO NOT WANT because Jesus was made poor, that I through His poverty might have abundance. Jesus came that I might have life and have it more abundantly (Psalm 23:1; 2 Corinthians 8:9; John 10:10).

I have received the gift of righteousness, therefore, I do reign as a king in life by Jesus Christ (Romans 5:17).

The Lord has pleasure in the prosperity of His servant, and Abraham's blessings are mine (Psalm 35:27; Galatians 3:14).

I seek first the kingdom of God and His righteousness, so all things I need are added unto me (Matthew 6:32-33).

God, Who did not withhold or spare even His own Son, but gave Him up for us all, freely gives me all other things (Romans 8:32, *The Amplified Bible*).

The powerful, active, living Word of God is always on my lips. I meditate on it day and night that I may observe and do what is written in it. As a result, I'm prosperous and successful. And since I'm willing and obedient, I eat the good of the land (Hebrews 4:12; Joshua 1:8; Isaiah 1:19).

The Lord teaches me to profit and leads me by the way I should go. Blessings are coming upon me and overtaking me, as the Lord daily loads me with benefits (Isaiah 48:17; Deuteronomy 28:2; Psalm 68:19).

I have faith and do not doubt. Whatever I ask for in prayer, really believing, I receive from the Lord, Who is able to do exceeding abundantly above all that I ask or think (Matthew 21:21-22, *The Amplified Bible*; Ephesians 3:20).

I ask and it is given to me; I seek and find; I knock and the door is opened to me (Matthew 7:7-11).

I am the righteousness of God in Christ Jesus. So the wealth of the sinner, which is laid up for me, is finding its way into my hands. God is giving sinners the task of gathering and storing up wealth to hand it over to me (2 Corinthians 5:21; Proverbs 13:22, *The Amplified Bible*; Ecclesiastes 2:26, *New International Version*).

The Lord goes before me, levels the mountains, and makes the crooked places straight. He gives me the treasures of darkness and hidden riches of secret places (Isaiah 45:2-3, *The Amplified Bible*).

God gives me seed because I'm a sower. He will multiply the seed I have sown (1 Corinthians 9:8-11, *The Amplified Bible*).

I prosper in every way and my body keeps well (3 John 2, *The Amplified Bible*).

Prosperity Scriptures

QUICK REFERENCE LIST

Prosperity
Is a Covenant Blessing—Chapter 3

Prosperity
Is Wisdom, Favor and Success—Chapter 4
Wisdom

Favor

Prosperity
Is Provision, Protection and Well-being
Chapter 5
Provision

*Prosperity
Promises*

What Jesus Said
About Prosperity—Chapter 7

Scripture
Quick Reference
List

Prosperity Promises
WORD/SCRIPTURE INDEX

gift (s)

give (n), (r), (s), (th), (ing), gave

increase (d), (th), (ing)

*Prosperity
Promises*

Psalm 115:11-16, p. 15
2 Corinthians 9:8-11, p. 111

overflow (ing)
Deuteronomy 28:1-14, p. 68
Psalm 65:4-13, p. 123
Proverbs 3:9-10, p. 38
Matthew 12:34-37, p. 251
John 10:10, p. 226

plenteous, plentiful
Deuteronomy 28:1-14, p. 68
Psalm 37:11, p. 178
Isaiah 30:23, p. 127

plenty
Leviticus 26:3-5, p. 24
Proverbs 3:9-10, p. 38
Acts 14:17, p. 20

prosper (ed), (ing), (s)
Genesis 39:2-4, p. 102
Genesis 39:21-23, p. 103
Deuteronomy 7:13, p. 2
Deuteronomy 29:9, p. 74
Joshua 1:7-8, p. 30
1 Kings 2:3, p. 31
2 Kings 18:7, p. 118
1 Chronicles 22:13, p. 32
2 Chronicles 20:20, p. 33
2 Chronicles 26:5, p. 34
2 Chronicles 31:21, p. 35
Job 1:10, p. 147

Word/
Scripture Index

prosperity

prosperous

sow (ed), (n), (s), (eth), (ing)

succeed (ed)
Genesis 39:2-4, p. 102
Deuteronomy 29:9, p. 74
Joshua 1:7-8, p. 30
2 Kings 18:7, p. 118
1 Chronicles 22:13, p. 32
Psalm 37:3-11, p. 5
Isaiah 48:15, 17, p. 129
Isaiah 54:17, p. 153

success
Genesis 39:2-4, p. 102
Joshua 1:7-8, p. 30
2 Kings 18:7, p. 118

tithe
Leviticus 27:30, p. 25
Malachi 3:10-12, p. 48

wealth (y)
Genesis 13:2, 5-6, 14-17, p. 58
Deuteronomy 8:17-18, p. 65
1 Chronicles 29:11-12, p. 3
2 Chronicles 1:12, p. 89
2 Chronicles 17:3-6, p. 120
2 Chronicles 29:2, 32:27-29, p. 141
Psalm 112:1-9, p. 77
Proverbs 3:9-10, p. 38
Proverbs 8:17-21, p. 17
Proverbs 10:2-6, p. 39
Proverbs 10:22, p. 168
Proverbs 13:11-13, p. 42
Proverbs 13:22, p. 179

Word/
Scripture Index

wisdom

Prayer for Salvation
and Baptism in the Holy Spirit

Heavenly Father, I come to You in the Name of Jesus. Your Word says, "*Whosoever shall call on the name of the Lord shall be saved*" (Acts 2:21). I am calling on You. I pray and ask Jesus to come into my heart and be Lord over my life according to Romans 10:9-10. "*If thou shalt confess with thy mouth the Lord Jesus, and shalt believe in thine heart that God hath raised him from the dead, thou shalt be saved.*" I do that now. I confess that Jesus is Lord, and I believe in my heart that God raised Him from the dead.

I am now reborn! I am a Christian—a child of Almighty God! I am saved! You also said in Your Word, "*If ye then, being evil, know how to give good gifts unto your children: HOW MUCH MORE shall your heavenly Father give the Holy Spirit to them that ask him?*" (Luke 11:13). I'm also asking You to fill me with the Holy Spirit. Holy Spirit, rise up within me as I praise God. I fully expect to speak with other tongues as You give me the utterance (Acts 2:4).

Begin to praise God for filling you with the Holy Spirit. Speak those words and syllables you receive—not in your own language, but the language given to you by the Holy Spirit. You have to use your own voice. God will not force you to speak. Worship and praise Him in your heavenly language—in other tongues.

Continue with the blessing God has given you and pray in tongues each day.

You are a born-again, Spirit-filled believer. You'll never be the same!

Find a good Word of God preaching church, and become a part of a church family who will love and care for you as you love and care for them.

We need to be hooked up to each other. It increases our strength in God. It's God's plan for us.

About the Authors

Kenneth and Gloria Copeland are the best-selling authors of more than 60 books such as the popular *Walk With God*, *How to Discipline Your Flesh* and *God's Will for You*. Together they have co-authored other books including *Healing Promises* and the popular devotional *From Faith to Faith—A Daily Guide to Victory*. As founders of Kenneth Copeland Ministries in Fort Worth, Texas, Kenneth and Gloria are in their 30th year of circling the globe with the uncompromised Word of God, preaching and teaching a lifestyle of victory for every Christian.

Their daily and weekly *Believer's Voice of Victory* television broadcasts now air on nearly 500 stations around the world, and their *Believer's Voice of Victory* and *Shout!* magazines are sent to nearly 700,000 adults and children worldwide. Their international prison ministry reaches an average of 60,000 new inmates every year and receives more than 30,000 pieces of correspondence each month. With offices and staff in the United States, Canada, England, Australia, South Africa and Ukraine, Kenneth and Gloria's teaching materials—books, magazines, audio and videotapes—have been translated into at least 22 languages to reach the world with the love of God.

Books by Kenneth Copeland

* A Ceremony of Marriage
  A Matter of Choice
  Covenant of Blood
  Faith and Patience—The Power Twins
  Family Promises
* Freedom From Fear
  From Faith to Faith—A Daily Guide to Victory
  Giving and Receiving
  Healing Promises
  Honor—Walking in Honesty, Truth & Integrity
  How to Conquer Strife
  How to Discipline Your Flesh
  How to Receive Communion
  Love Never Fails
  Managing God's Mutual Funds
* Now Are We in Christ Jesus
* Our Covenant With God
* Prayer—Your Foundation for Success
  Prosperity Promises
  Prosperity: The Choice Is Yours
  Rumors of War   .
* Sensitivity of Heart
  Six Steps to Excellence in Ministry
  Sorrow Not! Winning Over Grief and Sorrow
* The Decision Is Yours
* The Force of Faith
* The Force of Righteousness
  The Image of God in You
  The Laws of Prosperity
* The Mercy of God
  The Miraculous Realm of God's Love
  The Outpouring of the Spirit—The Result of Prayer
* The Power of the Tongue
  The Power to Be Forever Free
  The Troublemaker
* The Winning Attitude
* Welcome to the Family
* You Are Healed!
  Your Right-Standing With God

*Available in Spanish

Books by Gloria Copeland

* And Jesus Healed Them All
  Are You Ready?
  Build Your Financial Foundation
  Build Yourself an Ark
  Family Promises
  Fight On!
  From Faith to Faith—A Daily Guide to Victory
  God's Prescription for Divine Health
  God's Success Formula
  God's Will for You
  God's Will for Your Healing
  God's Will Is Prosperity
* God's Will Is the Holy Spirit
* Harvest of Health
  Healing Promises
  Living Contact
* Love—The Secret to Your Success
  No Deposit—No Return
  Pleasing the Father
  Pressing In—It's Worth It All
  The Power to Live a New Life
  The Unbeatable Spirit of Faith
* Walk in the Spirit
  Walk With God
  Well Worth the Wait

*Available in Spanish

Other Books Published by KCP

Heirs Together by Mac Hammond
John G. Lake—His Life, His Sermons,
       His Boldness of Faith
The New Testament in Modern Speech
       by Richard Francis Weymouth
Real People. Real Needs. Real Victories.
Winning the World by Mac Hammond

Other Books Published by Heirborne

Baby Praise
The SWORD

World Offices
of Kenneth Copeland Ministries

For more information about KCM and a free catalog, please write the office nearest you:

Kenneth Copeland Ministries
Fort Worth, Texas 76192-0001

Kenneth Copeland
Locked Bag 2600
Mansfield Delivery Centre
QUEENSLAND 4122
AUSTRALIA

Kenneth Copeland
Post Office Box 15
BATH
BA1 1GD
ENGLAND

Kenneth Copeland
Private Bag X 909
FOUNTAINEBLEAU
2032
REPUBLIC OF SOUTH AFRICA

Kenneth Copeland
Post Office Box 378
Surrey
BRITISH COLUMBIA
V3T 5B6
CANADA

220123 MINSK
REPUBLIC OF BELARUS
Post Office 123
P/B 35
Kenneth Copeland Ministries